THE FRUITFUL LIFE

Dr. David Chapman

The Fruitful Life

Dr. David Chapman

Printed in the United States of America. All rights reserved under International Copyright Law. Contents and/or cover may not be reproduced in whole or in part in any form without the expressed written consent of the Publisher.

All Bible quotations are from the King James Version unless otherwise noted.

Copyright © 2020

TRU Publishing
1726 S. 1st Ave.
Safford, Arizona 85546

Table of Contents

1. Conflict: Spirit vs. Flesh 6
2. Abiding in the Vine 14
3. The Fruit of the Spirit 24
4. The Sower, The Seed And The Ground 34
5. The Fruit of Love 51
6. The Fruit of Joy 68
7. The Fruit of Peace 78
8. The Fruit Longsuffering 88
9. The Fruit of Kindness 98
10. The Fruit of Goodness 107
11. The Fruit of Faithfulness 118
12. The Fruit of Gentleness 128
13. The Fruit of Self-Control 137

Dedication

I want to dedicate this book to my beautiful wife Debbie. She is the hardest working person I know (she's the best Veterinarian in the state of Arizona – in my unbiased opinion). But she also goes out of her way to be kind. She has grown immensely in the fruit of the Spirit over the past few years. She inspires me every day and without her I wouldn't be able to fulfill my mission.

Introduction

Through my many years of ministry I had always wanted to teach extensively on the fruit of the Spirit. The right time never seemed to come until August of 2019. Through the course of six months I taught a series on *The Fruitful Life*, which included the nine fruit of the Spirit. During that same time I also wrote this book. God has used this word in my own life to provoke me to greater fruitfulness. Further, I witnessed the spiritual growth in my congregation. It is my prayer that as you read this book that God would work in you a greater capacity for the fruitful life.

1. Conflict: Spirit vs. Flesh

Every Christian wants to live *the fruitful life*. But this does not happen by coincidence or by accident. Every believer has to contend with the nature of the flesh (the selfish orientation) in order to live victoriously in the Spirit. Paul describes the battle this way in Romans 7:

> **Romans 7:15 (NLT) I don't really understand myself, for I want to do what is right, but I don't do it. Instead, I do what I hate.**

Part of living the fruitful life is understanding yourself. If you don't, you will surely sabotage yourself along the way. One cannot truly understand himself or herself without the help of the Holy Spirit. He is the one who enlightens and empowers. The fruitful life is one of introspection. The classical Greek philosopher Socrates said, "An unexamined life is not worth living." The Lord speaks into our lives many hard truths (see John 6). These dealings will often focus on the conflict that lies within us and will drive us into His presence to seek help.

Wanting to do what is right and live the fruitful life is a good place to start. But if we don't tap into the power of the Holy Spirit to begin living the overcoming life, we will continue to do what we hate and perpetuate the self-destructive patterns of the

> *As much as the devil is your greatest enemy, your flesh poses your greatest threat.*

past. Before we are saved, the human will is part of the fallen nature and without the convicting and drawing power of the Holy Spirit we cannot be born again. After conversion, we often fail in thinking that the will is strong enough to enforce our choices to do what is right. However, it's still not enough to will what is right. We must learn to live by the power of the Holy Spirit.

Galatians chapter 5 is where we will spend a good deal of time as we examine the fruit of the Spirit. But before Paul gets there, he makes some comments about the conflicting natures of the spirit and the flesh.

> **Galatians 5:16-17**
> **16 I say then: Walk in the Spirit, and you shall not fulfill the lust of the flesh.**
> **17 For the flesh lusts against the Spirit, and the Spirit against the flesh; and these are contrary to one another, so that you do not do the things that you wish.**

The original word for *contrary* (Gr. *antikeimai*) means to be "thoroughly irreconcilable." Your flesh will always oppose your desire to live a fruitful life in the Spirit. As much as the devil is your greatest enemy, your flesh poses your greatest threat. Clearly then, the goal becomes disabling or immobilizing the selfish nature in order to live by the power of the Spirit. Through the power of the resurrection, we can win this war.

Many marriages get dissolved on the basis of irreconcilable differences, but the spirit cannot get divorced from the flesh. The flesh must be crucified!

> **Galatians 5:24 And those who are Christ's have crucified the flesh with its passions and desires.**

The flesh will only cease to be an opponent after it goes back to the dust of the ground or at the time of the resurrection, whichever occurs first. You never reach a place where the flesh can be trusted. It must always be denied or its passions and desires will overrule the desires of the Spirit within you. Ultimately, this will stop you from accomplishing God's will for your life.

The Works of the Flesh

The works of the flesh are identifiable, or as the Scripture says, "[they] are evident." Paul listed them in this same passage to the Galatians (Galatians 5:19-21).

"Now the works of the flesh are evident..."

1. Adultery
2. Fornication
3. Uncleanness
4. Lewdness
5. Idolatry
6. Sorcery
7. Hatred
8. Contentions
9. Jealousies
10. Outbursts of wrath
11. Selfish ambitions
12. Dissensions
13. Heresies
14. Envy
15. Murders
16. Drunkenness
17. Revelries
18. And the like

As often as the case with the Bible, the list goes fittingly into subgroups. The 17 works of the flesh listed fit into four distinct categories:

1. Intimacy
2. Worship
3. Relationships
4. Boundaries

Intimacy	**Worship**
1. Adultery 2. Fornication (Gr. Porneia) 3. Uncleanness (Lust) 4. Lewdness (Filthiness)	5. Idolatry 6. Sorcery
Relationships	**Boundaries**
7. Hatred 8. Contentions 9. Jealousies 10. Outbursts of wrath 11. Selfish ambitions 12. Dissentions 13. Heresies (Divisions) 14. Envy 15. Murders	16. Drunkenness 17. Revelries

These are four areas of life that are major problem spots for people who are failing to live the fruitful life. Galatians 6:8 says, "For he who sows to his flesh will of the flesh reap corruption." When a person sows to the flesh in the areas of intimacy, worship, relationships and

> *When a person sows to the flesh in the areas of intimacy, worship, relationships and boundaries, they will reap corruption.*

boundaries, they will reap corruption. The Greek word (*phthora*) translated corruption means, "Destruction from internal corruption." It is too convenient and totally unhelpful to blame other people for the destructive conditions of an unfruitful life. The destruction first comes from within. When a person stops living to the flesh and instead lives by the Spirit, fruit is produced.

Examples:

Scenario	Work of Flesh	Fruit of Spirit
Your coworker lies about you at work and gets you in trouble.	**Outburst of wrath** You plan your revenge.	**Kindness** You go out of your way and do something nice for the person.
You have been celibate since you gave your life to Christ, but you're being tempted.	**Fornication** You give in to temptation because this person might be "the one."	**Self-control** You allow the Holy Spirit to strengthen you and walk away.
A promotion is possible at work but you'll have to compromise your values to get it.	**Selfish ambitions** Since you may never get the chance again you figure God will understand.	**Faithfulness** You keep your values and continue to do your job with excellence.
A family member hurt you a long	**Hatred** Your feelings tell	**Love** Forgiveness

time ago. Things have never been right with them since.	you to never let it go. The hurt from it has never healed so why should you forgive?	becomes a *choice* that you make because Christ forgave you of all your sin.
Someone at church offended you with something they said about you to a mutual friend.	**Dissention** Stop coming to church and tell others that this person is a liar and needs to fix their mess of a life.	**Gentleness** Go to the person in a gentle spirit and seek reconciliation since it's possibly a misunderstanding anyway.
You've been coming to church for 6 months and been sober for 4 months, but you lost your job and an old friend wants to go to your favorite bar.	**Drunkenness** It's been a tough day and everybody slips once in a while. That night restarts the old addiction and throws months of sobriety away.	**Self-control** Instead of yielding to the weakness of the flesh, you pray then call a friend from church that comes over to get you through the night.

It's important to understand that there is a difference between struggling with sin and living in sin. The latter is a choice while the former is a battle. It's easy to judge someone who is struggling, but God sees the heart. Make no mistake, every believer can overcome the sins of the flesh. We are no longer to be slaves to sin (Romans 6), but rather servants of righteousness. As you grow in Christ, you are able to put away the works of the flesh and come into maturity. This is the will of the Father for all His children.

As Christians, we are no longer to walk or live by the rule of the flesh, our *selfish orientation*. It is fallen and corrupt in nature from the time we enter the world. This happens because our original parent, Adam, disobeyed God in the Garden of Eden (Genesis 3). This is the reason a person must be born again before he or she can see the kingdom of God (John 3).

If you are reading this and have never been born again from above, right now turn your heart toward God and ask His forgiveness. Accept Jesus' death on the cross as penalty for your sin and confess with your mouth that Jesus Christ is raised from the dead and is your Lord. If you do this and mean it from your heart, you will be saved.

2. Abiding in the Vine

The purpose for this book is to give practical teaching on how we, as followers of Christ, can powerfully live the fruitful life through the Holy Spirit within us.

Jesus had much to say about His followers bearing fruit.

> **John 15:1-8**
> **1 "I am the true vine, and My Father is the vinedresser.**
> **2 Every branch in Me that does not bear fruit He takes away; and every branch that bears fruit He prunes, that it may bear more fruit.**
> **3 You are already clean because of the word which I have spoken to you.**
> **4 Abide in Me, and I in you. As the branch cannot bear fruit of itself, unless it abides in the vine, neither can you, unless you abide in Me.**
> **5 "I am the vine, you are the branches. He who abides in Me, and I in him, bears much fruit; for without Me you can do nothing.**
> **6 If anyone does not abide in Me, he is cast out as a branch and is withered; and they**

gather them and throw them into the fire, and they are burned.

7 If you abide in Me, and My words abide in you, you will ask what you desire, and it shall be done for you.

8 By this My Father is glorified, that you bear much fruit; so you will be My disciples.

When Jesus said, "I am the Vine," it was the seventh "I am" statement of Jesus in the gospel of John.

1. "**I am** the bread of life." (John 6:35, 41, 48, 51)
2. "**I am** the light of the world." (John 8:12)
3. "**I am** the door of the sheep." (John 10:7, 9)
4. "**I am** the good shepherd." (John 10:11, 14)
5. "**I am** the resurrection and the life." (John 11:25)
6. "**I am** the way, the truth, and the life." (John 14:6)
7. "**I am** the true vine." (John 15:1, 5)

In the Old Testament, God revealed Himself as "I AM" to Moses (Exodus 3:13-15). In the New Testament, Jesus reveals that He is the "I AM"

> *No one branch has any power that doesn't come from the Vine, Jesus.*

– "Before Abraham was, I AM" (John 8:58). The religious leaders rejected this proclamation from Jesus.

They picked up stones to throw at him (v 59). Even today, the religious world neglects to see Jesus for all He is. He fits somewhere in their Sunday School lesson, but He is not looked upon as the Almighty One.

The Father is the Vinedresser, or Gardener. We are the branches all joined to the same Vine – Jesus. Fruit is not the result of the greatness of the branches. All fruit is because of the greatness of the Vine. No one branch has any power that doesn't come from the Vine, Jesus. There are many talented and gifted people who are serving in the kingdom. But none of them have any spiritual ability to advance the kingdom of God outside of the union with the Vine.

Religion, apart from relationship, does good works in an effort to earn God's favor and often to draw recognition to oneself. Jesus confronted this problem with the Pharisees and religious leaders of His day. But only through relationship and union with the Vine are we able to do the Father's will and produce spiritual fruit that remains.

> *Chastening is not designed to "pay us back" but to bring us back.*

The Difference Between Pruning and Chastening

When we bear fruit, it pleases the Father. But being the perfect vinedresser that He is, He prunes us in order that we will bear more fruit in the season to come. Pruning is not always pleasant and is most often painful to the flesh. Chastening, although different from pruning, is similar in that the process isn't pleasant but the results produce fruit.

> **Hebrew 12:11 11 Now no chastening seems to be joyful for the present, but painful; nevertheless, afterward it yields the peaceable fruit of righteousness to those who have been trained by it.**

Chastening is specifically corrective towards behavior that doesn't please the Father. It is always done in love for the purpose of restoration. It is not designed to "pay us back" but to bring us back. Pruning is designed to remove unproductive activities or attitudes (branches), improve our overall walk with God, and direct new, healthy growth. Pruning happens because we are actually producing fruit and the Father wants our lives to be even more fruitful.

Here are the key differences between chastening and pruning:

Chastening	Pruning
• Chastening happens because we are doing something *wrong*.	• Pruning happens because we are doing something *right*.

• The goal of chastening is repentance to return us to fruitfulness.	• The goal of pruning is to produce greater surrender that we would bear even more fruit.

Of course, Satan always likes to hijack what God is doing and counterfeit it with something destructive. In this case it would be *condemnation*. The enemy wants us to believe that God is punishing us for something we did in the past — something that we've already repented of and been forgiven by God. But Romans 8:1 tells us that, "There is therefore now no condemnation to those who are in Christ Jesus." Pay special attention to the word "now" because there is a time association with these three activities. Condemnation is always associated with the *past*, while chastening is related to your present — what you are doing now, your present lifestyle. Pruning, as we've seen in John 15, is all about your future; God wants you to be more fruitful.

Activity:	Pruning	Chastening	Condemnation
Related to:	Future	Present	Past
Source:	God	God	Satan
Goal:	More Fruit	Repentance	Destruction

Areas for Pruning

Many people focus on the outward things when they think about going through a pruning from the Lord. Surely, this is sometimes the case. But there are many areas of our life where the Lord may deem needful to prune. Below are some examples.

Your Heart Attitudes
Without heart change, nothing else is going to matter much. The Lord wants to deal with the deep-seated issues of the soul. He will continue to prune our heart attitudes long after we *feel* we should have *arrived*. That's because the closer you get to Jesus, the more you will see in yourself that needs changed. The root issues of the heart are the primary focus of the Lord's pruning in the life of a believer. Allow the Lord to prune the branches of your heart so that you can be whole in Christ.

Your Circle
It's been said that a person becomes the average of the five people with whom the most time is spent. Proverbs 13:20 says, "He who walks with wise men will be wise, but the companion of fools will be destroyed." The Lord may need to prune out of your life the toxic relationships that are holding you back.

Your Habits
Simply stated, changing your habits will change your destiny. There's absolutely nothing that will impact

your life more than developing godly habits. The Lord will continue to prune us in this area as long as we're in this earth journey. Hit and miss devotional time with the Lord will make you like the wave of the sea and keep you from receiving anything from the Lord (James 1:6-8). Brain science tells us that the human brain operates in 21-day cycles and that it takes three consecutive cycles to form a habit. This would be 63 days. Basically, you are able to change your entire destiny in two months if you are committed.

Your Scenery
Sometimes you're doing the *right* thing in the *wrong* place. Geography plays a role in what we accomplish. The Lord may need to prune your scenery in order for you to bear more fruit. Sometimes you've accomplished all that you can in a certain place. Just make sure that you allow the Holy Spirit to make that determination so that you don't fall into *the grass is greener on the other side of the fence* trap. Don't stay somewhere out of obligation to man when God has clearly directed otherwise.

Remember the four areas in which the works of the flesh operate:

1. Intimacy
2. Worship
3. Relationship

4. Boundaries

Pruning will certainly occur in these key areas in order to bring us into a fruitful life.

Abiding

We must learn to abide in Jesus, the Vine. The same sap that is in the Vine, flows into the branch. Because of this living union, we are able to produce fruit. All the branch has to do is abide. The word *abide* comes from the Greek word *menō* and shows up 120 times in the New Testament. The word means, "To dwell, to continue to be present, to remain." In his writings, John uses the word a total of 55 times. In essence, it means to sustain unbroken fellowship. Living the fruitful life is completely dependent upon this unbroken fellowship with Jesus.

Peter, in his second epistle describes this beautiful union.

> **2 Peter 1:4 by which have been given to us exceedingly great and precious promises, that through these you may be partakers of the divine nature, having escaped the corruption that is in the world through lust.**

The branch becomes a partaker of the nature of the Vine through this union. To be a partaker means, "to be a joint-participant." The branch by itself is a lifeless entity and only has life when it is connected to the Vine. Through participation with the Vine, growth occurs and fruit is produced. All true believers are branches of the same tree. We are all one through the Vine.

Similarly, Paul wrote in 1 Corinthians 6:17, "But he who is joined to the Lord is one spirit with Him." The Greek word translated *joined* is *kollaó* and literally means, "to be glued together." This is why the Bible tells us that nothing can separate us from His love (Romans 8:38).

> *The sap that is in the Vine cannot flow into the branch without the function of abiding.*

To *abide* is a relationship basic. Jesus said, "If you abide in My word, you are My disciples indeed. And you shall know the truth, and the truth shall make you free" (John 8:31-32). Without getting into the Word, the relationship with the Master becomes stagnant. The sap that is in the Vine cannot flow into the branch without the function of abiding. But by continuing in the Word, the truth is able to heal our heart and renew our mind. The truth must become our spiritual DNA in that it is imbedded into our personality and thought patterns.

James 1:21 Therefore lay aside all filthiness and overflow of wickedness, and receive with meekness the implanted word, which is able to save your souls.

This isn't speaking of our eternal salvation, for that is not a process. Eternal salvation is based completely on the finished work of Christ on the cross. This is referring to the wholeness of salvation that indeed is a process that comes from abiding in the Word and allowing it to become implanted into our identity.

3. The Fruit of the Spirit

There are several groups of spiritual attributes listed in the New Testament. There are groups of ministries, gifts, spiritual manifestations, etc. It cannot be definitely said that the groups or lists are exhaustive. In most cases they should be seen as representative. Below are some of the groups of spiritual attributes listed in the New Testament.

Ministries (Ephesians 4:11)
1. Apostle
2. Prophet
3. Evangelist
4. Pastor
5. Teacher
Spiritual Manifestations (1 Corinthians 12:4-11)
1. Word of wisdom
2. Word of knowledge
3. Faith
4. Healings
5. Working of miracles
6. Prophecy
7. Discerning of spirits

8. Different kinds of tongues
9. Interpretation of tongues

Motivational Gifts (Romans 12:4-8)

1. Prophecy
2. Serving
3. Teaching
4. Exhortation (Encouragement)
5. Giving
6. Leadership
7. Mercy

It is the same Holy Spirit who is working in these many different ways. There are diverse expressions of the Holy Spirit because He is God and His supply is unlimited. God uses people in many different ways. What is different about the nine fruit of the Spirit is that while no one person has all of the attributes on any of the above lists, each follower of Jesus may have all nine of the fruit.

In our Galatians 5 passage, Paul comes to the matter of the fruitful life, powered by the personality of the Holy Spirit. It should be understood that there are many characteristics and attributes of the Holy Spirit. Not all of them could be considered positive. As examples, the Holy Spirit exhibits attributes such as correction and judgment. But when it comes to the fruit of the Spirit in the life of the believer, only positive attributes are listed.

> **Galatians 5:22-23**
> **22 But the fruit of the Spirit is love, joy, peace, longsuffering, kindness, goodness, faithfulness,**
> **23 gentleness, self-control. Against such there is no law.**

The Nine Fruit of the Spirit

1. Love
2. Joy
3. Peace
4. Longsuffering
5. Kindness
6. Goodness
7. Faithfulness
8. Gentleness
9. Self-Control

Upon examination, it would seem that there are three groups within this list of nine fruit – each springing from the same root, the Holy Spirit.

Group 1	Group 2	Group 3
1. Love	4. Longsuffering	7. Faithfulness
2. Joy	5. Kindness	8. Gentleness

3. Peace	6. Goodness	9. Self-Control
These reflect communion and intimacy with God.	These reflect our interactions with others.	These reflect our temperament in difficult circumstances.

It's important to note that Paul uses the singular *fruit* instead of the plural *fruits*. Organically, they are connected and make up a whole, as opposed to being isolated fruits. As an example, without love, how can one show kindness and without kindness, what value has love.

> ***Simply stated, the fruit of the Spirit is the character and nature of Jesus.***

Against such there is no law

"But the fruit of the Spirit is... Against such there is no law."

The Galatians had a terrible struggle with legalism. There are many such similar churches today. Everything is about rules and outward

> ***God's Word can only be obeyed by the power of the Holy Spirit.***

performance. Paul makes another strike against such attitudes here as it relates to the fruit of the Spirit. He declares that there is no law that can regulate the power of these attributes known as the fruit of the Spirit.

The fruitful life is so much more fulfilling than the legalistic life. The former comes from an abiding relationship with Jesus while the latter is an outward adherence to a mixture of Bible laws and man-made rules. Even actual laws from the Bible were never intended to be obeyed from the power of human effort. God's Word can only be obeyed by the power of the Holy Spirit.

There are two kinds of legalism:

1. The kind of legalism that believes one must do works to *attain* salvation.
2. The kind of legalism that believes one must do works to *maintain* salvation.

The legalism that believes works is used to attain salvation is addressed in Ephesians 2:8-9:

> **For by grace you have been saved through faith, and that not of yourselves; it is the gift of God, not of works, lest anyone should boast.**

Further, Romans 3:20 says that, "By the works of the law no flesh will be justified in His sight."

The legalism that believes works is used to maintain salvation is addressed in Galatians 3:3, 5:

> **3 Are you so foolish? Having begun in the Spirit, are you now being made perfect by the flesh?**
> **5 Therefore He who supplies the Spirit to you and works miracles among you, does He do it by the works of the law, or by the hearing of faith?**

In effect, both types of legalism are subtle. Both preach Jesus, but it's not Jesus plus nothing. Instead, it's Jesus plus works. Fruit doesn't come through the works of the law. The fruitful life happens because of abiding in the Vine – Jesus. Fruit is an overflow of relationship with Jesus. Good works will be produced because of the fruit in the Spirit-filled believer's life.

***Love* will conquer the coldness of legalism every time.**

> Jesus said that we would be known as His followers by our love for one another (John 13:35), not by the charitable works that we do. In fact, 1 Corinthians 13 tells us that without love, all those charitable deeds mean nothing.

***Joy* will triumph over the sadness of legalism without fail.**

> One thing conspicuously absent from the religious leaders of Jesus' day was joy. If you are in a church where there is no joy, you're likely in a legalistic church. Some people think that a sad face is more holy. Jesus said, "Therefore you now have sorrow; but I will see you again and your heart will rejoice, and your joy no one will take from you" (John 16:22).

***Peace* will lift you above the anxiety of legalistic performance.**

> With legalism you can never do enough to achieve peace within. Performance based Christianity will always leave you short. About the Pharisees, Jesus said, "You crush people with unbearable religious demands, and you never lift a finger to ease the burden" (Luke 11:46 NLT). True peace comes from personal relationship with Jesus.

***Longsuffering* will endure long after legalism has failed in the hour of need.**

> Legalism has a man-powered battery. It is operated by will power. Paul said it this way: "I want to do what is right, but I don't do it. Instead, I do what I hate" (Romans 7:15 NLT). The fruit of longsuffering comes from the power of the Spirit within who won't allow us

to surrender to the circumstances or succumb under trial.

Kindness will always prevail against the harshness of legalism.

> Religion drives people away with harsh demands to conform. With legalism, mercy is reserved for those who *deserve* it. Quite an oxymoron. Kindness by nature is merciful. Legalism always wants the upper hand in order to control people. Pharisees think that the worse you can make people feel about themselves, the more control you have over them. But have you ever heard the phrase, "Kill them with kindness"? Kindness disarms people who are ready to defend themselves. Proverbs 15:1 says, "A gentle answer deflects anger." Kindness always prevails.

Goodness never fails to undo the cruel misdeeds of legalism.

> Goodness is the quality that builds others up, but bad religion does nothing more than tears people down. The general public has the perception that if you want to feel bad about yourself just go to church. Every time you go to church, try to find at least five people to encourage by saying something positive.

Faithfulness will keep you moving forward when legalism will keep you stuck.

Legalism simulates the characteristics of faithfulness, but ultimately fails. True faithfulness will not only persevere, but will produce change in doing so. I know legalistic people who are holding down the fort and they haven't spiritually grown in 20 years.

Gentleness has compassionate healing power for those who've been wounded by the cruelty of legalism.

Jesus was meek and gentle towards those who were hurting. Yet bad religion has driven God's sheep away from the church. They are all around us in a wounded state. Jesus said to forgive seventy times seven (Matthew 18:22) but legalism has no capacity to forgive even once.

Self-control is available by the power of the Spirit instead of the weak and fruitless will power of legalism.

Self-control is not a control that's powered by *self*, but it's the power of the Spirit within a person to deny the flesh. Rules alone don't stop destructive behavior. This was proven in the very beginning with Adam and the tree of the knowledge of god and evil (Genesis 3). Religion has virtually no power to help a person overcome addictions. Addictions will continue as long as self-control is powered by human effort. The Holy Spirit will give you power to say no to the destructive forces of temptation.

4. The Sower, The Seed And The Ground

In Matthew 13:18-23, Jesus talked about four kinds of hearts related to the "word of the Kingdom." Only one of these four types of hearts goes on to live the fruitful life.

> **Matthew 13:18-23**
> **18 "Therefore hear the parable of the sower:**
> **19 When anyone hears the word of the kingdom, and does not understand it, then the wicked one comes and snatches away what was sown in his heart. This is he who received seed by the wayside.**
> **20 But he who received the seed on stony places, this is he who hears the word and immediately receives it with joy;**
> **21 yet he has no root in himself, but endures only for a while. For when tribulation or persecution arises because of the word, immediately he stumbles.**
> **22 Now he who received seed among the thorns is he who hears the word, and the cares**

> of this world and the deceitfulness of riches choke the word, and he becomes unfruitful."
>
> **23** But he who received seed on the good ground is he who hears the word and understands it, who indeed bears fruit and produces: some a hundredfold, some sixty, some thirty."

The Wayside Heart

> When anyone hears the word of the kingdom, and does not understand it, then the wicked one comes and snatches away what was sown in his heart. This is he who received seed by the wayside.

When this person hears the Word of God, he allows the devil to *snatch* the Word out of his heart. The word "snatch" in the Greek means, "to seize upon openly with force." These are those who *mentally* agree with the Word, and may even *emotionally* respond, but don't allow the Word to get into their hearts. Satan is able to attack them quickly with temptation and pull them away.

Frequently, in the church that I pastor, I encounter individuals who receive the seed of the Word this way. It's heartbreaking to watch people go right back to their mess without being truly converted. Without Jesus, you know they don't stand a chance.

In John chapter two, there's an example of many Jewish people believing in Jesus when they saw the miracles that He performed. But something interesting happened – Jesus did not commit Himself to them. How could it be that people made a public commitment to Jesus but He did make a corresponding commitment to them? Quite simply, Jesus knew that they were insincere in their commitment.

> **John 2:23-25**
> **23 Now when He was in Jerusalem at the Passover, during the feast, many believed in His name when they saw the signs which He did.**
> **24 But Jesus did not commit Himself to them, because He knew all men,**
> **25 and had no need that anyone should testify of man, for He knew what was in man.**

Jesus knows the heart condition of every person that fits the description of the wayside believer. Their belief is superficial and easily defeated by the enemy.

The Stony Ground Heart

But he who received the seed on stony places, this is he who hears the word and immediately receives it with joy; yet he has no root in himself, but endures only for a while. For when tribulation or persecution arises because of the word, immediately he stumbles.

When this person hears the Word of God, he immediately responds *outwardly* on a superficial level. This person gets excited about what he has heard, but doesn't allow the Word to take root in his heart. Notice that the root of God's Word must be in one's self. No one can do this for you. Spiritual counselors and godly mentors are great to have, but ultimately the responsibility rests with each individual. This person allowed hardships and persecution to get in the way of following Jesus. As a consequence, the stony heart person only endures for a while. He is not prepared for the persecution that will arise for the Word's sake.

Make no mistake... when you openly declare God's Word, be prepared to be attacked. Notice that this person *immediately* receives the Word, and *immediately* falls away. Impulsiveness will lead to short-term commitment.

> *When you openly declare God's Word, be prepared to be attacked.*

Jesus taught that to follow Him one needed to count the cost (Luke 14:28). In the year 2019, one in nine

Christians worldwide experiences severe persecution for following Christ.

If there is one thing that Satan fears it is a follower of Jesus who gets rooted and grounded in the Word of God. This is why he attacks early and often whenever a person decides to make a commitment to the Word. Getting rooted is critical to being built up. Without the root system a tree cannot stand. The roots of a tree spread twice as deep and twice as wide as the height and circumference of the tree's branches.

The original word for "stumbles" (*skandalizó*) in this verse means, "To fall into a trap." Troubles and persecutions are just traps from the enemy to steal the Word of God out of your heart. As Proverbs 4:23 says, "Above all else, guard your heart, for everything you do flows from it (NIV)."

The Thorny Ground Heart

> **Now he who received seed among the thorns is he who hears the word, and the cares of this world and the deceitfulness of riches choke the word, and he becomes unfruitful.**

This person hears the Word of God, but does not allow it to penetrate and deal with the heart issues to root out the thorns that are already there. He appears to be making progress. But when life's pressures come, the thorns that are already there begin to surface. The cares of this world choke out the Word of God. The Greek word for "choke" (*sumpnigó*) means, "To choke like weeds do to a plant."

This person becomes unfruitful, which means that at one time there was the beginning stage of fruitfulness. It's always encouraging to see a person begin to be fruitful. Others can invest so much in this person's growth. But ultimately, there will come a time when the individual must press through and overcome the barriers of growth. Luke's version of this parable says he *brings no fruit to maturity* (Luke 8:14). Whatever fruit is produced is short-lived and incomplete.

The deceitfulness of riches is a trap that is easy to fall into, given the materialistic society in which we live. But a person cannot serve both God and mammon (Gr. "the treasure a person trusts in") and be fruitful (Matthew 6:24). Giving up heavenly treasure for short-term materialistic gain is the most near-sighted decision a person can make. If you put God first in your life, He will provide all that you need.

There comes a point in every believer's walk with Jesus where you have to count the cost, take up your cross and follow Him. Jesus clearly taught that the way to eternal life was narrow and difficult (Matthew 7:14).

You cannot take along all of the baggage of the world. The cares of this life and the pursuit of material things will eventually choke out the Word of God.

> **Hebrews 12:1-2**
> **1 Therefore we also, since we are surrounded by so great a cloud of witnesses, let us lay aside every weight, and the sin which so easily ensnares us, and let us run with endurance the race that is set before us,**
> **2 looking unto Jesus, the author and finisher of our faith, who for the joy that was set before Him endured the cross, despising the shame, and has sat down at the right hand of the throne of God.**

It is not only the sins that will keep a person defeated but also the extra weight that one tries to carry. Eventually, these cares will choke out the Word of God and bring defeat.

The Good Ground Heart

> **But he who received seed on the good ground is he who hears the word and understands it, who indeed bears fruit and produces: some a hundredfold, some sixty, some thirty.**

This person hears the Word of God and receives it with meekness (James 1:21). He applies it to understanding, allowing the Word to change the inward man. He allows it to renew his mind to begin a new pattern of thinking (Romans 12:2). The Greek word for "receive" means, "to embrace with agreement and obedience." It is not enough to hear and receive the Word of God; one must also obey the Word by putting it into practice.

James 1:22 says, "But be doers of the word, and not hearers only, deceiving yourselves." When we act on the Word, real change and lasting fruit are produced in our lives. One notable difference are our vocabulary changes – we no longer go around talking defeat, but confidence is in our voice as we declare that we can do all things through Christ Jesus who strengthens us. Instead of needing ministered *to* all of the time, we now become the one who ministers to others.

> *Sadly, Jesus said that only one-fourth of those who hear the Word of God will actually live the fruitful life.*

Sadly, Jesus said that only one-fourth of those who hear the Word of God will actually live the fruitful life. If you plant yourself in a place where there are other growing trees, it increases the chances that you will also grow and produce fruit. I have heard that a tree planted in a forest with other trees will tap into the existing root system and grow much faster than a tree planted off by itself. It is crucial to be part of a church where the Word of God is being taught and practiced.

Rooted – Guard Your Heart

The fruitful life is one that happens because of being rooted. Without being rooted, one cannot be built up. Roots take time. A person cannot plant a peach pit and expect fruit the first year. It takes three to four years before it starts to produce fruit. That's not to say that a new Christian cannot demonstrate the fruits of salvation. But there is a discipleship process needed to bring forth fruit to maturity. It takes time to become established.

> **Colossians 2:7 rooted and built up in Him and established in the faith, as you have been taught.**

Not only are we encouraged to develop good roots in the Word, but we are also warned to guard against negative roots that can contaminate the soil of our heart.

> **Hebrews 12:15 Looking carefully lest anyone fall short of the grace of God; lest any root of bitterness springing up cause trouble, and by this many become defiled.**

There are several key words in this verse that merit our attention.

"Looking carefully" – (Gr. *episkopeó*) means, "Total focus." This matter demands greater attention than a casual observance. The Bible tells us that it's the *little foxes* that spoil the vine (Song 2:15). The believer cannot afford to have blind spots that result in bitterness within the soul. Bitterness is a poison that can creep into a person's heart when unguarded.

"Fall short" – (Gr. *hustereó*) means, "to be tardy." It's possible to be tardy (delayed, overdue, late) to the grace of God. When you hold onto things and refuse to let them go, it causes you to be out of sync with God's timing. God's delays are not denials, but man-made delays will lengthen your trials. Remember when Israel was coming out of Egypt? They technically had a 30-day trip, but by God's design it was supposed to take two years; instead it took 40 years. The generation that came out of Egypt fell short of the Promised Land.

> *As a rule of the Spirit, you must into every day with the intentionality of not being offended.*

"Bitterness" – (Gr. *pikria*) means, "Harshness, resentment." Life is too short to be ruled by harshness and resentment. Prolonged bitterness produces callousness within the heart, causing one to become insensitive and unfeeling. This heart condition grieves the Holy Spirit and the person becomes unfruitful. As a rule of the Spirit, you must into every day with the intentionality of not being offended. Psalm 119:165 says, "Great peace have they which love thy law: and nothing shall offend them" (KJV).

"Trouble" – (Gr. *enochleó*) means, "To excite, disturb, annoy," and also brings the word picture, "To be carried along by a raging mob." The *momentum* of bitterness will carry you along involuntarily, taking you into further and more trouble. If you've ever been shopping on Black Friday, perhaps you've been carried along by a mob of shoppers. The feeling is one of total loss of control. You end up going places you had no intention of going. That's the kind of trouble that allowing a root of bitterness produces.

"Defiled" – (Gr. *miainó*) means, "To be tainted with dye at the source so that everything passing through becomes stained." The same word is used in Titus 1:15: *"To the pure, all things are pure, but to the defiled and unbelieving, nothing is pure; but both their minds and their consciences are defiled."* This defilement will cause your mind (filter) and your conscience (rationalizations) to be defective. The contamination from this type of exposure cannot only affect one's soul, but also the physical health of an individual.

What Do Roots Do?

1. **Absorb water, minerals, and nutrients and pass them through to the plant.**

   The spiritual nourishment that comes through the Word of God will be passed through to every area of your life when you get rooted in the Word. A Christian cannot survive without this nourishment. Jesus said, "Man shall not live by bread alone, but by every word that proceeds from the mouth of God" (Matthew 4:4).

   The path to a healthy soul, mind and emotional state is through the Word of God. The Word becomes a surgical tool in the hand of God, the Great Physician (Hebrews 4:12). He will deal with every area of our life – one at a time.

   > *Without being rooted in the Word, there's no spiritual anchor in your soul (soil) to keep you upright in times of trouble.*

   On the other hand, when you have a root of bitterness, you are absorbing and passing through your spirit the contamination and poison of unforgiveness. Are you allowing yourself to soak up negativity?

Consider how it is affecting your life – garbage in, garbage out.

2. Anchor the plant so that it doesn't fall over.

The Word of God gives you the stability needed to overcome in a life filled with unexpected ups and downs. The Word provides the foundation needed to withstand the storms of life (Matthew 7:24-27). God can turn around what may appear to be the fatal fall of a believer, when he is rooted in the Word. Proverbs 24:16 says, "For the righteous falls seven times and rises again." Being rooted will cause you to rise again.

When you invest time in devotions, Bible reading, prayer, coming to church and Bible Study, you might ask why is this important? You are getting anchored for the storm and the value of an anchor is known only in a storm. Don't see God through the filter of your circumstances, but see your circumstances through the filter of the Word of God.

Without being rooted in the Word, there's no spiritual anchor in your soul (soil) to keep you upright in times of trouble. My job as a pastor is to be more of a *root* inspector than a fruit inspector. Even the most spiritual person can allow their strength to become their weakness if he doesn't stay anchored in the Word. Elijah on Mt. Carmel declared, "I'm the only one left." His statement was one of victory, as he trusted God to defeat the prophets of Baal. But later, on the run from Jezebel and in the cave, he cried, "I'm the only one left." But this time it was a declaration of defeat. Elijah was failing to stay rooted in the Word of God.

3. Stores extra food for future use.

Your future is greatly shaped by getting rooted in the Word of God. In the parable of the sower, the *stony ground heart* appeared to have a great future, but he had no depth of root and only survived a little while. There was nothing to sustain him when the scorching sun (the circumstances) beat down on him.

When I was saved and called into the ministry at the age of 20, I spent about five years in the Word of God day and night. Those thousands of hours in the Word stored up spiritual food for me that I have been nourished with many times through the years. I have remained a student of the Word, but there have been times when I wasn't able to devote the same amount of time. It's important to understand your seasons. Paul told Timothy, "Timothy, my son, in accordance with the prophecies previously made concerning you, that by them you fight the good fight" (1 Timothy 1:18 NAS).

The same principle is true on the negative side. If you only realized how much the root of bitterness or the root of jealousy had to do with your future, you'd change your food source and get into the Word of God. These bitter roots will contaminate your future endeavors and relationships. It is a *prophecy* over your life for trouble.

There was a season in my life about 20 years ago when I prayed to God every day for 6 months to kill me. I had become bitter and angry at the way life worked out for me. Much like Jeremiah (20:7-10) I felt deceived but God's Word in me brought me through that season.

4. **Secrete compounds into the soil that help protect the plant from disease.**

There's something life changing about being in an environment that's charged with God's Spirit and God's Word. Collectively, we all release positive compounds into our environment and culture that help protect the Lord's plants from spiritual disease. Isaiah 61:3 calls us "the planting of the Lord."

The roots of anger, bitterness, jealousy and other destructive attitudes will defile the environment and cause things to be unhealthy. The two most important things in church life are: 1) the People; and 2) the Culture. Buildings are irrelevant. An environment of love will bring salvation and healing, but a spiritually toxic environment will defile and bring disease (spiritual, emotional and physical).

The first triad of love, joy and peace reflect communion and intimacy with God.

5. The Fruit of Love

*Galatians 5:22 But the fruit of the Spirit is **love**, joy, peace, longsuffering, kindness, goodness, faithfulness, 23 gentleness, self-control. Against such there is no law.*

> **Word Gem: Gr. *agapé* (ἀγάπη) – translated *love*, "A divine love that prefers others above self."**

The word *love* is in the NKJV Bible 504 times – 267 in the Old Testament and 237 in the New Testament. *Agapē* is the most common word in the New Testament translated *love* (142 times). *Agapē* love is a *discriminating love* – it prefers and chooses others above self.

In the principles of Bible interpretation, there is such a thing as the *law of first mention*. This means that the first time a word or subject is mentioned in the Bible, it carries significant weight in how it's interpreted in the following uses throughout Scripture. The first time love is mentioned is in Genesis.

> **Genesis 22:2 Then He said, "Take now your son, your only son Isaac, whom you <u>love</u>, and go to the land of Moriah, and offer him there as a burnt offering on one of the mountains of which I shall tell you."**

The first time the word love is used is in the context of being tested. Could Abraham truly love his son Isaac, but still offer him to God? Ultimately, this was a prototype of God sending His only begotten Son to die on the cross for the sins of the world. Abraham trusted God and passed the test. As a result, he was incredibly blessed and his descendants became as numerous as the stars of the sky. Are there areas in your life where you feel God is testing your love? Whatever you surrender to Him ultimately goes to a greater level. Whatever and whoever you love here in this life, must never outweigh your love and devotion to God.

> *Love without priorities is nothing more than a feeling.*

Remember, *agapē* is all about making a choice. Love without priorities is nothing more than a feeling.

The worship song *Reckless Love* has become popular recently and also controversial because some argue that God's love could never be reckless. However, the etymology of the word is "to take action without regard to the consequences to yourself." This is the type of love that Jesus displayed on the cross.

> **John 3:16 For God so loved the world that He gave His only begotten Son, that whoever believes in Him should not perish but have everlasting life.**

Types of Love

There are two main words translated "love" in the New Testament:

1) *Agapē* – a self-sacrificing love
2) *Phileō* – a companionable love

A third word, *Eros* (not used in NT), means self-satisfaction/gratification.

Three Types of Love

Type of love: Eros
Objective: *My* happiness
Description: Though *Eros* is directed towards another, it actually has *self* in mind. For example: "I love you because you make *me* happy."

Example:

A 19-year-old male, James, begins dating an 18-year-old female, Kari. After one month, James begins pressuring for the relationship to become physical. He insists that he loves Kari and because of his insistence she complies, even though she wanted to wait. One month later, because of her Christian faith, Kari tells James that she can no longer engage in physical intimacy. He gets very angry and immediately breaks off the relationship. In this example, James "loved" Kari because she was giving him what he wanted. It was nothing more than eros.

Type of love: Phileō

Objective: *Our* happiness

Description: There is a mutuality aspect. Greek scholar Kenneth Wuest said, "It is a love that is called out of one's heart as a response to the pleasure one takes in a person or object." This love works as long as both parties are happy.

Example:

Danny and Adam met in high school and always had a lot in common. They both liked sports and liked to work on cars. As they got older, they remained good friends. Once, they both liked the same girl and quit speaking to each other for a while. But later the friendship rekindled when Danny got Adam a job at his company because he knew that Adam could land an important account. Danny and Adam's entire friendship was based off having things in common and what they could do for one another. Any time this was tested, as with the girl, the friendship halted. While they cared about one another, it was always on a phileō level.

Type of love: Agapē

Objective: *Your* happiness

Description: Agapē is an actionable love that chooses someone else's needs and desires above one's own. Its primary concern is the happiness of another.

Example:

Emily was a 6-year-old little girl suffering from a rare life threatening disease. Her only chance of recovery appeared to be a blood transfusion from her 8-year-old brother Eric, who had somehow survived the same disease and had developed the antibodies needed to combat the illness. The doctor explained the situation to her brother, and asked the little boy if he would be willing to give his blood to his sister. He hesitated for only a moment before saying, "Yes, I'll do it if it will save her." He lay in bed next to his sister as the transfusion progressed. He looked up at the doctor and asked with a trembling voice, "Will I start to die right away?" The little boy thought that giving his blood meant that he would die. This is a commonly used example of selfless love – agapē love.

> **Agapē is not something we *fall into* – e.g., "I fell in love." It is something we *choose into*.**

Love Is More Than An Ideal

I remember when I first starting pastoring. I had a general love for the people in my congregation, but I was mainly serving out of my love for God. As time passed, the love that I had for the people I was serving grew and became strong. This happened by a work of the Holy Spirit, but also through the different experiences we shared. Those experiences included times of celebration, but also adversities and hardships. Love has to be more than a concept or idea. It must be walked out in practical living.

Love God With All Your Heart

One day an expert in religious law tried to trap Jesus with a question about which was the most important commandment in the Law (Matthew 22:35-36). Jesus answered with the following reply:

> **Matthew 22:37-38**
> **37 Jesus said to him, "You shall love the LORD your God with all your heart, with all your soul, and with all your mind.**

38 This is the first and great commandment. 39 And the second is like it: You shall love your neighbor as yourself."

The Christian life is not one of casual affection. Jesus describes an all-consuming love that happens in the heart and life of His followers. This is the kind of love that cannot be produced by human effort. Its origin is divine. Truly, we love Him because He first loved us (1 John 4:19). When the miracle of life happens inside the human heart, it fills us with a passionate love for our Savior. This love must be guarded because there are many opponents to this condition – none greater than the opponent of apathy. If loving the Lord in this manner is the greatest commandment of all, then by consequence, a failure to do so must be the greatest sin that a Christian can commit.

Then, Jesus gives a second commandment: "You shall love your neighbor as yourself." What does it mean to love my neighbor as myself? By nature, each of us has a self-preservation mentality. This is the old nature, of course. The second commandment is like the first in that it's through His love in us that we are able to love others. Everyone has a need to be loved, but that doesn't make everyone lovable. It's through the supernatural power of God's love that we are able to love people with the same kind of care as we give ourselves. This is actually not just a New Testament concept, as the Law said the same thing.

> **Leviticus 19:18 You shall not take vengeance, nor bear any grudge against the children of your people, but you shall love your neighbor as yourself: I am the LORD.**

Jesus said that we'd be known as His disciples because we have love for one another (John 13:35). There's a real emphasis on the *one another*. Sometimes it's easier to show love for strangers and the less fortunate. We can drop off our care package and be on our way. But those around us – one another – know how to push our buttons and disappoint us. This is where the quality of our love is tested.

> **John 13:34 A new commandment I give to you, that you love one another; as I have loved you, that you also love one another. 35 By this all will know that you are My disciples, if you have love for one another."**

Love Your Enemies

Not only are we supposed to love one another – fellow believers, but we are also supposed to love our enemies. When the Jews read the commandment in Leviticus 19:18 love your neighbor as yourself, they wrongly inferred that they must therefore hate their enemies. Jesus made it clear that this was not the case.

> **Matthew 5:43-44**
> **43 You have heard that it was said, 'You shall love your neighbor and hate your enemy.'**
> **44 But I say to you, love your enemies, bless those who curse you, do good to those who hate you, and pray for those who spitefully use you and persecute you.**

Examples of Agapē Love

- A husband loves his wife with a sacrificial love – figuratively and if need be, literally laying done his life for her (Ephesians 5:25, 33).

- A pastor/shepherd loves his flock and cares for their needs. When trouble comes, he does not run for he isn't a hireling (John 10:12-13, 1 Peter 5:2-3).

- Fellow believers love one another by the bond of the Holy Spirit (John 13:34-35).

- Parents love their children deeply enough to sacrifice for their well-being and to correct them when they're wrong (Proverbs 22:6, Ephesians 6:4).

- A follower of Jesus is verbally persecuted because of his faith. In response to the persecution, he performs an act of kindness as an act of love to his enemy (Matthew 5:44).

Don't Let Your Love Grow Lukewarm or Cold

In the letter of Jesus to the church at Ephesus in the book of Revelation, Jesus chastised the Ephesian believers for forsaking their first love. They were still doing the works, but their passion and devotion to Jesus had crept into a stagnant state. He said this to them, "Nevertheless I have this against you, that you have left your first love" (Revelation 2:4).

It's so easy to get caught up going through the motions without the heartfelt devotion to Jesus. That's not to say that there won't be times when you go forward with nothing but faith in the absence of feelings. Just remember, love is a decision, not a feeling.

One of the primary ways that a believer allows his love to grow cold is by entertaining sin. Jesus said, "Sin will be rampant everywhere, and the love of many will grow cold" (Matthew 24:12 NLT). He said this about the end times and those days are upon us. There are so many sinful choices that are vying for the believer's heart.

As Proverbs 4:23 says, "Keep your heart with all diligence." Regularly examine your motives for the things you do in the area of service to others. Ask God to keep your motives pure and to refresh and increase your love for Him and others.

The Love Chapter

1 Corinthians 13 is known as the love chapter. It gives a beautiful description of Agapē love.

> **1 Corinthians 13:4-8**
> **4 Love suffers long and is kind; love does not envy; love does not parade itself, is not puffed up;**
> **5 does not behave rudely, does not seek its own, is not provoked, thinks no evil;**
> **6 does not rejoice in iniquity, but rejoices in the truth;**
> **7 bears all things, believes all things, hopes all things, endures all things.**
> **8 Love never fails.**

How Does Love Act?

1. **[Suffers long]** Love is willing to suffer a long time in the interests of another. God is longsuffering toward us, not willing that any should perish (2 Peter 3:9). Love is patient. We want people to change overnight, but it doesn't always work that way. This means

you're slow to anger; you endure personal wrongs without retaliating. You bear with others' imperfections, faults, and differences. You give them time to change.

2. **[Kind]** Love is kind in the way it treats others. Kindness is very much about how you make people feel. People usually forget what you *say*; they frequently forget what you *do* for them; but they never forget how you made them *feel*.

    - The word for *kind* can also be translated *useful*. Find ways to be useful in people's lives.
    - Kindness motivates others toward positive change.

8 Things that love is NOT (3-10):

3. **[Does not envy]** Love is not envious or jealous when others do well or succeed. Christians are not to be in competition with one another. Envy and jealousy are works of the flesh (Galatians 5:20-21).

    - Envy caused Cain to murder Abel (Genesis 4:3-8).

- Envy caused Joseph's brothers to see Joseph into slavery (Genesis 37).

4. **[Does not parade itself]** Love does not parade around making it known to others all of its good deeds. Service performed out of genuine love does not need a photo shoot. The Pharisees liked for all of their good deeds to be seen by men (Matthew 6:1). If the Lord so chooses that your good deeds go unnoticed, rejoice, for you may have the greatest reward of all if you keep your heart right.

5. **[Not puffed up]** Love doesn't get lifted up in pride, causing you to think you're better than others. Remember, this is sandwiched between two chapters on the gifts of the Spirit. It's easy to get caught up in pride when the Lord uses you.

6. **[Does not behave rudely]** Love does not behave rudely, but is polite. We should stop and think about how much of our testimony we lose when we behave rudely, even for a moment (traffic, checkout lines, food service, etc.). I know some wonderful people who seem to always find themselves in some sort of confrontation or altercation. Love does not needlessly offend.

7. **[Does not seek its own]** Love cares about the needs and feelings of others and not just its own. Remember, agape love discriminates against itself in the best interests of others. If your life is filled with problems, the best thing you can do is get involved in someone else's problems.

8. **[Not provoked]** Love doesn't have a short fuse that is easily provoked. It's important to remember that our fight is not with flesh and blood. People may be the ones pushing your buttons, but the nature of the battle is spiritual (Ephesians 6:10-17). Satan will use the aggravations to get you distracted and in the flesh.

9. **[Thinks no evil]** Love doesn't plot revenge and think evil towards others. Love is not always suspicious of others. Love has to have a predominant place in your thought life. Let's suppose you were the landlord of an apartment complex and rented 80% of your apartments to drug dealers, thugs, thieves and criminals and the other 20% to normal, good people. After a short period of time, which group do you think would run the other one off? Of course, the 80% bad would run off the 20% good. You are the landlord of your mind. Stop renting space in your mind to evil!

Many translations render this phrase: "keeps no record of wrongs." When you begin record keeping in your mind of every wrong committed against you, you have already failed at love.

10. **[Does not rejoice in iniquity]** Love isn't glad when enemies fall because of sin. Proverbs 24:17: *Do not rejoice when your enemy falls, and do not let your heart be glad when he stumbles*. Instead, we should always be seeking to restore those who've fallen (Galatians 6:1).

11. **[Rejoices in the truth]** Love rejoices and celebrates in the understanding of truth. The Bible says that the truth should always be spoken in love (Ephesians 4:15). The truth spoken harshly can cause great harm. Sometimes people aren't ready to hear the truth. When God opens their heart to hear, it's truly a time to rejoice because the truth can set them free (John 8:32). Love will confront with sensitivity and correct because it cares deeply and knows that sin destroys.

12. **[Bears all things]** Love is able to bear up under any circumstance. There's no circumstance that love cannot overcome. The Greek word for *bears* (*stegó*) can also

be translated "to cover over." This is why the Bible tells us "love covers a multitude of sins (1 Peter 4:8). "Love stands in the presence of a fault, with a finger on her lip" (Charles Spurgeon).

13. **[Believes all things]** Love believes the best about others. Frequently, people judge others by their actions, but themselves by their intentions. This is not encouraging us to be gullible, but to trust unless there's a good reason not to. Some times you will get burned.

> *Love believes the best about others.*

14. **[Hopes all things]** Love is not pessimistic, but is filled with optimism. Love has a lasting hope for favorable outcomes. Love will lift someone from the despair of hopelessness. There are so many hopeless people in our world and just one touch of God's love can turn things around. You just might be the vessel that God wants to use to make that happen.

15. **[Endures all things]** Love endures when every other strategy fails. Our strategy to build this church is to love people with God's love. The Greek word for *endure* means, "To remain under the load for as

long as it takes." There are very few things that endure till the end, but I know that God's Word does (1 Peter 1:25), the true believer does (Matthew 24:13) and *agape* love endures forever.

16. **LOVE NEVER FAILS**. If *love never fails*, wouldn't that mean that all failure is ultimately a failure to love? I realize how simplistic that sounds, but it's also true. If we choose to love in every situation, we will ultimately prevail. There may be temporal loss, but in the Father's eyes there can be no failure when His love is shown.

6. The Fruit of Joy

*Galatians 5:22 But the fruit of the Spirit is love, **joy**, peace, longsuffering, kindness, goodness, faithfulness, 23 gentleness, self-control. Against such there is no law.*

> **Word Gem: Gr. *chara* (χαρά) – translated *joy*, "The awareness of God's grace and favor; cheerfulness, calm delight."**

The word *joy* is in the NKJV Bible 192 times – 127 in the Old Testament and 65 in the New Testament. The Psalmist (40) and Isaiah (30) are the most prolific users of the word. When all the variations of the word are counted (joy, joyful, rejoice), there are over 400 instances (ESV); by contrast the word happiness is found only 25 times.

The first time that the word joy is used in relation to God in the New King James version of the Bible is Deuteronomy 28.

Deuteronomy 28:47-48

47 "Because you did not serve the Lord your God with joy and gladness of heart, for the abundance of everything,

48 therefore you shall serve your enemies, whom the Lord will send against you, in hunger, in thirst, in nakedness, and in need of everything; and He will put a yoke of iron on your neck until He has destroyed you.

The Lord places so much emphasis on serving Him with joy. The Israelites had physical enemies, but Christians have spiritual enemies. When we allow our joy to be stolen it gives Satan the upper hand and causes the yoke of oppression on our lives. Joy is spiritual force that helps us dominate in the arena of spiritual warfare. As we will discover, joy is not something outside our control. It is not determined by circumstances. We can have joy because the victory has already been won through the cross and the resurrection. We are not fighting to get to the victory, but from the *place* of victory. Guarding our joy in battle is one of the ways we do that.

> *Joy is spiritual force that helps us dominate in the arena of spiritual warfare.*

Christians should be the most joyful people on the face of the earth. Happiness can be very superficial and fleeting if stimulated by outward conditions. Joy is not a secondary thought to God; it is an essential ingredient to the Christian life. Even in the painful seasons of life, joy becomes a sustaining force.

Joy vs. Happiness

There is a difference between *joy* and *happiness,* although at times they can be synonymous. The latter is mostly dependent upon favorable circumstances or *happenings*, while the former is an inward condition of the heart.

Happiness	Joy
• Based on favorable circumstances or what *happens*	• Based on inward attributes
• Outward and often superficial	• Independent of external circumstances or what *happens*
• Fleeting in nature	• Direct source: Holy Spirit
• Like a *thermometer* just registering the conditions	• Lasting in nature
	• Like a *thermostat* that controls the conditions

No One Can Take It From You

Jesus said that He gave us a joy that no one can take from us. He never said that our happiness could never be taken. There are circumstances in life that certainly disrupt the condition of our happiness, but no one can rob your joy without your permission.

> **John 16:22 Therefore you too have grief now; but I will see you again, and your heart will rejoice, and no one will take your joy away from you.**

Even though joy is a sustainable force, we must guard our hearts in order to sustain it. If we don't guard our hearts, we can allow the joy of the Lord to dissipate or become suppressed. After a time of estrangement from the Lord, David prayed, "Restore to me the joy of Your salvation" (Psalm 51:12).

> *It is more important to praise God when you don't feel like it than at any other time.*

Rejoice!

> **Philippians 4:4 Rejoice in the Lord always. Again I will say, rejoice!**

We can keep our joy active by praising God. The book of Philippians tells us to "Rejoice in the Lord always and again I say rejoice!" (Philippians 4:4). What exactly does it mean to rejoice? To borrow a computer term, essentially, to rejoice means to *reboot* your joy. When you reboot a computer it closes all of the programs and applications and restarts the operating system. This is necessary at times because of the build up of random, unimportant, and temporary data bogging down your device or computer. Basically, it causes all of your memory and processing resources to become drained. Rebooting flushes all of that out of the system.

Similarly, our lives get cluttered and fragmented and it begins to put a drain on our joy. According to the meaning of the Greek word translated *rejoice* (*chairó*), the act of rejoicing means to "lean in and become connected to God's grace – to be consciously glad." This is done through the act of praising God.

It is more important to praise God when you don't feel like it than at any other time. In fact, David used to speak to himself when he was down and remind himself to praise God.

> **Psalm 42:5 (ESV) Why are you cast down, O my soul, and why are you in turmoil within**

> **me? Hope in God; for I shall again praise him, my salvation.**

Paul felt like it was so important to rejoice that he essentially said, if it doesn't work the first time, do it again! As many times as necessary, flush the negativity out of your soul and fix your praise on God for the good things He's done in your life. When you are short on joy, get into God's presence because in His presence there is fullness of joy.

> **Psalm 16:11 You will show me the path of life; In Your presence is fullness of joy; At Your right hand are pleasures forevermore.**

There are many verses in the New Testament regarding the practice of rejoicing:

> **1 Thessalonians 5:16 Rejoice always.**
> **2 Corinthians 6:10 As sorrowful, yet always rejoicing...**
> **Romans 12:15 Rejoice with those who rejoice...**

Joy In Hardship

> **James 1:2-3**
> **2 My brethren, count it all joy when you fall into various trials.**

3 knowing that the testing of your faith produces patience [endurance].

The reason that we are able to count it all joy when we are tested is because we *know* that God is doing something greater and the trial is just a means to an end. God is building endurance within us – a necessary ingredient to success. The emphasis of the word *count* means to *have a leading thought*. In other words, go into the situation with a determined mind that you're not going to let it steal your joy.

So many people instead choose to get mad at God when they fall into some sort of trial. By the way, the Greek word for *fall* means, "to be totally surrounded by." That means there's not a simple way out. What will determine your breakthrough more than anything else is "counting it all joy." There are going to be times in life when we are surrounded by trouble. Jesus said that as long as we are in the world it would be inevitable.

> **John 16:33 In the world you will have tribulation; but be of good cheer, I have overcome the world**

In this verse we see the *external* condition (tribulation) vs. the *internal* condition (good cheer).

Tribulation	Good Cheer
• External	• Internal
• Gr. "To be under pressure, hemmed in, no way of escape"	• Gr. "Confident, courageous, unafraid"

Jesus said, "I have overcome (*nikao*) the world." This verb is written in the Perfect Tense, meaning completed action in past time with present continual results. In other words, we already know the outcome. Whatever it is that you may be going through, God is in control. He is faithful and He will make a way of deliverance (1 Corinthians 10:13).

The olive press (or the winepress) was a place where pressure was applied to the olive (or grape) in order to produce oil (or wine). But too much pressure would have a detrimental effect, causing the seed to be crushed and bitterness to be released. In order to apply the right amount of pressure and not the full weight of the pressers, a rope was hung from a beam above and the presser would lift part of his body weight to lessen the pressure upon the olives. When we find ourselves (metaphorically) in the olive press we must trust God that He will apply only the right amount of pressure in

> *We must trust God that He will apply only the right amount of pressure.*

order to produce the oil without the bitterness.

Anytime that bitterness is produced in the soul, it is never because of a dealing from God. He will never permit us to be tested beyond our ability to overcome (1 Corinthians 10:13). Bitterness is a tool of Satan to rob us of our joy. The hardships of life are not designed to strip us of our joy, but we must certainly become more focused and thankful to maintain our joy during those times.

Rejoice That Your Names Are Written In Heaven

Jesus taught a valuable principle in Luke chapter 10. After sending out the 70 disciples to spread the Good News of the kingdom, they returned with joy because of the success of their ministry and their authority over demons (v 17). But Jesus told them not to base their joy on these outward signs, but instead base their joy on their relationship with God – that their names were written in heaven.

> **Luke 10:20 Nevertheless do not rejoice in this, that the spirits are subject to you, but rather rejoice because your names are written in heaven.**

Ministry success is awesome, but keep your joy centered on Jesus! Your identity cannot be limited to what you *do*. Your identity must be based on *who you are*. God places significant value on each of His children and our joy must be relationship-based, not works-based. Like all of the fruit, joy comes through abiding in the Vine – Jesus (John 15).

Consider the prodigal son and his older brother (Luke 15). It was the Father's delight to restore his son who was lost. There was no penalty to pay before the party began. It was a time of joyous celebration. Nothing had been earned. Everything had been given. As Christians, we cannot do anything to merit this great joy. It's based on relationship with the Father. On the other hand, the older son had remained faithful and served attentively. Yet he stood outside of joy looking in. Works alone cannot produce the kind of joy God wants to give.

> ***Your identity cannot be limited to what you do.***

Religion wants to dispense some form of artificial joy to its adherents. In other words, put on a fake smile and pretend to be joyful because that's what's expected. The reality is that this type of behavior is counterproductive to the body of Christ. Nothing that's truly from God can be produced where the recipients aren't being real or genuine.

7. The Fruit of Peace

*Galatians 5:22 But the fruit of the Spirit is love, joy, **peace**, longsuffering, kindness, goodness, faithfulness, 23 gentleness, self-control. Against such there is no law.*

> **Word Gem: Gr. *eiréné* (εἰρήνη)** – translated *peace*, "to join, tie together into a whole – properly, wholeness, i.e. when all essential parts are joined together; peace."

The word *peace* is in the NKJV Bible 397 times – 288 in the Old Testament and 98 in the New Testament. The main original word in the Old Testament Hebrew is *shalom*. Shalom is word that's rich in meaning. The word means, "completeness or wholeness, peace, contentment, safety and prosperity."

As it relates to the New Testament Greek, by looking at the original word for *peace* (*eiréné*) it can be seen that peace is a holistic condition – a joining together of life's disconnected parts. This is not to imply that all areas of your life have to be in order before you can experience peace.

Confusion is the opposite of peace and God is not the author of confusion (1 Corinthians 14:33). Always second-guessing your decisions can rob you of God's peace. When it comes to receiving direction from the Lord, people tend to over-complicate things by trying to understand every aspect of the direction. When God called Abraham he was told to "Get out" from where he was. That part was clear and certain. But the rest of the direction was, "to a land that I will show you." While the former is certain, the latter is uncertain and without clarity.

> **Genesis 12:1 Now the LORD had said to Abram: "Get out of your country, From your family And from your father's house, To a land that I will show you.**

In most cases, God will progressively reveal the details of His plan after you obey the parts that you have clear conviction about. This is where God's peace comes in and confusion is not allowed to arrest your progress. But when you get hung up on trying to understand parts that haven't been revealed it will cripple you from obeying the part that is clear.

I like to use sports metaphors when I'm preaching. The apostle Paul liked to do that as well – wrestling, running, boxing and such. Like sporting events today, the ones in the first century had umpires and referees. In his letter to the Colossians, he referred to the peace of God being like an *umpire* in your heart.

> **Colossians 3:15 (AMP) And let the peace (soul harmony which comes) from Christ rule (act as umpire continually/ be the controlling factor) in your hearts [deciding and settling with finality all questions that arise in your minds, in that peaceful state] to which as [members of Christ's] one body you were also called [to live]. And be thankful (appreciative), [giving praise to God always].**

Never make a major decision when you don't have God's peace. Even if every thing lines up circumstantially, if you don't have peace, "pump the brakes." I once made a major move in my life without God's peace and I regretted it horribly. It was related to accepting the pastorate of another church in a different state. On the surface, it checked all the boxes. There were several outward confirmations. My house sold the first day the sign went in the ground. But there was only one problem

> *Never make a major decision when you don't have God's peace.*

and I kept ignoring it. I didn't have any peace from God about the decision. In fact, I had turbulence in my spirit. But I kept suppressing it and focusing on the confirmations. I learned a major lesson through that experience, which I was fortunate to live through, but with great suffering. Never give outward signs or confirmations a higher ranking than God's peace. In fact, don't do anything major in your life without God's peace.

Lots of people have married the wrong person because they didn't want to cancel the wedding and disappoint other people. Deep down, they knew it was wrong, but they ignored the commotion in their heart. Others have taken new jobs that paid a dollar more an hour, but at the expense of their peace. Listen to God and let His peace rule in your heart.

False Peace

Is there such a thing as *false peace*? Can people convince themselves or become duped into thinking they are right with God when they aren't? The Bible tells us that the human heart is very deceitful (Jeremiah 17:9) and because of this, a person can experience a false peace or a false sense of security.

Deuteronomy 29:18-19 (NASB)

> **18 so that there will not be among you a man or woman, or family or tribe, whose heart turns away today from the LORD our God, to go and serve the gods of those nations; that there will not be among you a root bearing poisonous fruit and wormwood.**
>
> **19 It shall be when he hears the words of this curse, that he will boast, saying, <u>"I have peace though I walk in the stubbornness of my heart</u> in order to destroy the watered land with the dry."**

The stubbornness of the human heart will never produce peace. When a person rejects the counsel of God, the first step taken is to rationalize the decision. This can produce false assurances and ultimately result in great harm. When we again and again refuse to heed the Lord's voice in our lives, there is nothing left for God to do but to turn us over to our own stubbornness. *"But My people would not heed My voice, And Israel would have none of Me. So I gave them over to their own stubborn heart, to walk in their own counsels"* (Psalm 81:11-12).

> *Make sure that the peace you feel about something lines up with the Word*

Verify

In order to protect yourself from trusting in a false peace, make sure to verify your peace with Scripture because the Holy Spirit and the Word of God are always in agreement. When people make claims to have God's peace about something, but it contradicts God's Word, it's clearly an error.

In addition to making sure that the peace you feel about something lines up with the Word, also make sure that your conscience is clear. It's impossible to have the genuine peace of God without a clear conscience. Peace, the Word and a clear conscience are like a three-fold cord that will protect you in your decision-making.

A Three-Fold Cord
1. Peace from the Holy Spirit
2. Verification from the Word
3. Clear conscience

Surpasses Understanding

Perhaps the greatest revelation of God's peace in the Bible is found in the book of Philippians.

> **Philippians 4:6-8**
> **6 Be anxious for nothing, but in everything by prayer and supplication, with thanksgiving, let your requests be made known to God;**

7 and the peace of God, which surpasses all understanding, will guard your hearts and minds through Christ Jesus.

8 Finally, brethren, whatever things are true, whatever things are noble, whatever things are just, whatever things are pure, whatever things are lovely, whatever things are of good report, if there is any virtue and if there is anything praiseworthy—meditate on these things.

In verses 6 and 7, Paul compares and contrasts anxiety and peace. He tells us how to get rid of the former and gain the latter. While the word for *peace* (*eiréné*) means, "to join together into a whole," the word for *anxious* (*merimnaó*) means, "to be divided into parts, going different directions, or coming apart." Anxiety will rob a person of person of their wholeness and peace. The surest way to overcome anxiety is to follow the instructions of verse 6 and take everything to God in prayer – with thanksgiving.

> *When we take things to the Lord in prayer we will trade our anxiety for peace.*

When we take things to the Lord in prayer we will trade our anxiety for peace. Through His peace, we can be whole instead of coming apart. Peace will guard our hearts and minds.

God can give you peace in your spirit that your natural mind cannot comprehend or understand. Peace provides the believer with a knowing from the Holy Spirit that goes beyond what the understanding of the mind can provide. Have you ever simply known that a prayer was answered, even though the actual manifestation hadn't

> *Satan is always trying to get God's people offended because it will steal your peace.*

occurred yet? This is the power of God's peace. I've had this experience more times than I can count. God drops a peace into my spirit about a matter of concern and prayer. From then on, I simply know that it's worked out. I thank and praise God until the breakthrough happens. Sometimes the situation looks impossible, but I still have this knowing through the peace of God that assures me of the outcome. And without fail, God comes through at just the perfect time.

Live Peaceably

> **Romans 12:18 If it is possible, as much as depends on you, live peaceably with all men.**

In some cases, people won't allow you to be peaceable. But when possible, do all that you can to live in peace with people – especially God's children. You don't have to agree with everything they do to be at peace.

Satan is always trying to get God's people offended because it will steal your peace. Psalm 119:165 says, "Great peace have they which love thy law: and nothing shall offend them."

Jesus said: "Blessed are the peacemakers, for they shall be called sons of God" (Matthew 5:9). Peacemakers differ from peacekeepers in that the former are willing to be confrontational with the goal of establishing true peace instead of just maintaining the façade of peace.

The second triad of longsuffering, kindness and goodness reflect our interactions with others.

8. The Fruit Longsuffering

*Galatians 5:22 But the fruit of the Spirit is love, joy, peace, **longsuffering**, kindness, goodness, faithfulness, 23 gentleness, self-control. Against such there is no law.*

> **Word Gem:** Gr. *makrothumia* (μακροθυμία) – translated *longsuffering*. This is a compound word: *makros* means "long" and *thumos* means "temper." A person with *makrothumia* is long tempered and has steadfastness and staying power. This person has self-restraint and does not hastily retaliate a wrong. This comes only from the Holy Spirit.

The word *longsuffering* is in the NKJV Bible 16 times – 3 in the Old Testament and 13 in the New Testament. The word *makrothumia* is in the Greek New Testament 14 times. Many translations of verse 22 use the word *patience* instead of longsuffering.

Not many people get excited at the prospect of doing a Bible study on the subject of longsuffering. Some think that if you ignore such difficult subjects then life will be more pleasant. The reality is that every life comes with times of suffering – some to a greater and some to a lesser degree. Jesus said that while in this world, we would have tribulation (John 16:33). It's been said that life is 10% what happens to you and 90% how you respond. The fruit of longsuffering helps the believer to respond to life's suffering with the character of Christ.

Throughout the New Testament, we read words such as *endurance, patience* and *longsuffering*. While they are very synonymous, there are also distinctions.

Endurance	Longsuffering (Patience)
• Gr. *hupomonē* (32 times) • Compound word *hupó*, "under" and *ménō*, "remain, endure" • "The quality that doesn't surrender to circumstances or succumb under trial."	• Gr. *makrothumia* (14 times) • Compound word *makros*, "long" and *thumos*, "temper" • "To be long-tempered (as opposed to short-tempered). The self-restraint that does not hastily retaliate a wrong."

Based on these definitions, it seems that endurance is more applicable to the *circumstances* and longsuffering to dealing with *people*.

Circumstances	People
Endurance	Longsuffering

Ephesians 4:1-2
1 I, therefore, the prisoner of the Lord, beseech you to walk worthy of the calling with which you were called,
2 with all lowliness and gentleness, <u>with longsuffering, bearing with one another in love</u>.

I watched my dad go from being short-tempered when I was growing up to being long-tempered after he got saved. The transforming power of the gospel and the work of the Holy Spirit produce godly changes in our lives – even when those old behavior patterns have persisted for years.

> **Proverbs 15:18 (ESV) A hot-tempered man stirs up strife, but he who is slow to anger quiets contention.**

The self-restraint that goes with being longsuffering keeps you from responding hastily to people and making matters worse. A lack of restraint can make a person feel better in the moment, but ultimately cause much long-term harm. How many relationships have been severed because of the need to retaliate or speak one's mind?

Bible Examples of Being Longsuffering

Joseph

> **Genesis 50:15, 19-21**
> **15 When Joseph's brothers saw that their father was dead, they said, "Perhaps Joseph will hate us, and may actually repay us for all the evil which we did to him."**
> **19 Joseph said to them, "Do not be afraid, for am I in the place of God?**
> **20 But as for you, you meant evil against me; but God meant it for good, in order to bring it about as it is this day, to save many people alive.**
> **21 Now therefore, do not be afraid; I will provide for you and your little ones." And he comforted them and spoke kindly to them.**

Joseph was betrayed by his brothers because they were jealous of him and the favor he had from his father, Jacob. His coat of many colors meant that he loved Joseph most. Joseph was the eleventh of twelve sons and the first from his wife Rachel. As a boy, he had two dreams from God and in each of them, his brothers were bowing down to him. In the second dream, even his parents bowed to him. God was showing him that he would be a ruler some day.

In order for those dreams to come true, Joseph had to overcome tests related to circumstances and tests related to people. Remember, endurance is the character trait that deals with circumstances and longsuffering with people.

Joseph's Tests Related to Circumstances – Endurance	Joseph's Tests Related to People – Longsuffering
• Thrown into the pit • Sold into slavery • Thrown into prison • Ongoing imprisonment	• Jealousy from his brothers • Betrayal from his brothers • Temptation from Potiphar's wife • Forgotten by the cupbearer • Helping his brothers

Ultimately, it was a period of 13 years from the time Joseph had his dreams to when he became a ruler in Egypt, second to only Pharaoh. Further, it was 22 years after his dreams before his family came down to Egypt in the time of famine.

Joseph was a man of great character and excellent spirit. He overcame when few would have. Seeing his brothers again was the greatest challenge of his life. But he knew that what they meant for evil, God intended for good (Genesis 50:20). Because of the longsuffering of Joseph, the entire nation of Israel was spared and the lineage of the Messiah was preserved.

David

> **1 Samuel 24:4-7 (NIV)**
> **4 The men said, "This is the day the Lord spoke of when he said to you, 'I will give your enemy into your hands for you to deal with as you wish.'" Then David crept up unnoticed and cut off a corner of Saul's robe.**
> **5 Afterward, David was conscience-stricken for having cut off a corner of his robe.**
> **6 He said to his men, "The Lord forbid that I should do such a thing to my master, the Lord's anointed, or lay my hand on him; for he is the anointed of the Lord."**
> **7 With these words David sharply rebuked his men and did not allow them to attack Saul. And Saul left the cave and went his way.**

King Saul attempted to murder David no less than 12 times. He was very jealous of David and his military conquests. But it didn't start that way. David, as a youth, took out Goliath and saved Israel from defeat at the hands of the Philistines. Saul made David commander of the army and when the troops would return, the women would sing, "Saul has slain his thousands, And David his ten thousands" (1 Samuel 18). "And Saul was furious and resented this song" (1 Samuel 18:8 Berean Bible).

Relationships can get complicated very quickly, or over time. David had the anointing of God upon his life (1 Samuel 16), but it didn't mean he'd ascend straight to the throne. It was actually 14 years from the time David was anointed by Samuel until he became king of Judah and 21 years before he reigned over all Israel. But David had the opportunity to take shortcuts – to take out Saul and take the crown. But he knew that if God anointed him to be king, he would open the door when the time was right. As it is written in the Psalms, promotion comes from God.

> **Psalm 75:6-7**
> **6 Promotion comes neither from the east nor from the west nor from the south.**
> **7 But God is the Judge: He puts down one, and exalts another.**

When David had the chance to take Saul out, he was conscience-stricken. The fruit of longsuffering must rely on the conscience for guidance. What seems fair and just to the mind, may actually be against God's will. There were things that God was doing in David during this season of his life that could not have happened any other way.

To go from a shepherd boy to the king required longsuffering.

An Example of Failure – Moses

Moses, by definition was a humble and patient man of God. Beginning at the age of 80, he spent 40 years leading the nation of Israel through the wilderness. These people were full of unbelief and miserably complained the entire time. His patience was tested time and again, but he stood in the gap for Israel and

> *As God's representative, Moses acted in anger when the Lord wasn't angry, thus misrepresenting God to the people.*

reminded God that all the nations around them would see the failure if God started over with a new people.

After 40 years, Israel entered the Promised Land, but Moses was not permitted to enter. In many ways it seems unfair that Moses was forbidden, after all he'd been through. But there was an occasion when Moses was hot-tempered and misrepresented God to the people. This is what kept Moses out of the Promised Land. In Numbers 20, Moses was commanded by God to speak to the rock to bring water out of it. Instead, Moses angrily struck the rock twice and water gushed out. As God's representative, Moses acted in anger when the Lord wasn't angry, thus misrepresenting God to the people. As God's children and ambassadors it's important how we respond to people in unfavorable situations.

A failure to be longsuffering is what kept Moses from the greatest blessing of his life. Is this specific failure also preventing you from a great blessing?

Longsuffering in Ministry

Ministry is a response of obedience to the Lord's call. But the reality of ministry is dealing with people – all types of people. I always tell people called into the ministry that there are two things that can be counted on: 1) God is faithful, and 2) people will disappoint you. This is not meant to be critical, but honest. It is inevitable. Simply consider the ministry of Jesus and the call of the 12. Although He loved them with a perfect love, Jesus endured all their unbelief, ignorance, pride, narrow-mindedness and self-centeredness because He saw them for who they'd become, not just who they were at the time.

It's important to be longsuffering with those whom the Lord sends you to serve, or those whom He sends to help you. Typically, we have an idea in our mind of what those people will look like when they come. Unfortunately (but really, fortunately), the Lord usually has a different perspective. God doesn't look on the outward appearance but the heart (1 Samuel 16:7).

As leaders it's our greatest assignment to disciple and mentor people by seeing them through the lens of God's perspective. If you're going to be involved in any kind of ministry activity, you're going to need to be longsuffering.

God – the Model of Longsuffering

God is the ultimate example of longsuffering:

> **Romans 2:4 Or do you despise the riches of His goodness, forbearance, and longsuffering, not knowing that the goodness of God leads you to repentance?**

Whenever you're tempted to give up on someone, remember the riches of His goodness towards you. God has been longsuffering with you and His will is that you be likeminded and be longsuffering with others.

9. The Fruit of Kindness

*Galatians 5:22 But the fruit of the Spirit is love, joy, peace, longsuffering, **kindness**, goodness, faithfulness, 23 gentleness, self-control. Against such there is no law.*

> **Word Gem: Gr.** *chréstotés* (χρηστότης) – translated *kindness*, "useful, profitable; refers to meeting real needs, in God's way, in His timing."

The word *kindness* is in the NKJV Bible 46 times in 41 verses – 39 in the Old Testament and 7 in the New Testament.

This particular word (*chréstotés*) shows up 10 times in the New Testament. Interestingly, this word this word translated *kindness* isn't just a nice disposition. I think society often confuses kindness with politeness. Of course, politeness (being courteous, gracious and well-mannered) is an aspect of kindness, but kindness goes so much further in what it does for people. It's about being useful and meeting real needs of people, while doing it God's way.

Peter in his second letter instructed believers how to avoid being unproductive and unfruitful. In addition to other things, he wrote that we must add brotherly kindness to our godliness.

> **2 Peter 1:5-9**
>
> **5 But also for this very reason, giving all diligence, add to your faith virtue, to virtue knowledge,**
>
> **6 to knowledge self-control, to self-control perseverance, to perseverance godliness,**
>
> **7 <u>to godliness brotherly kindness, and to brotherly kindness love.</u>**
>
> **8 For if these things are yours and abound, you will be neither barren nor unfruitful in the knowledge of our Lord Jesus Christ.**
>
> **9 For he who lacks these things is shortsighted, even to blindness, and has forgotten that he was cleansed from his old sins.**

Some believe that it's enough to be godly – to abstain from sin, but God requires us to go further. There are some faithful and godly people who never give up that still don't experience the fruitful life. As Peter wrote, we need to keep adding these attributes of grace into our lives and conduct.

Faith → virtue → knowledge → self-control → perseverance → godliness → **kindness** → love

There's no way that we can be kind like our Lord in our own ability. The verse right in front of this passage tells us that we are "partakers of the divine nature" (v 4). Through the Holy Spirit in us, we are able to add these characteristics of Jesus to our daily lives, including kindness.

There's a lot of "religiously mean" people in the world and unfortunately, they draw a lot of attention. A failure to be kind to others is, as Peter wrote, to be *shortsighted*. Jesus encountered many religiously mean people when He was on the earth. Chief among them were the Pharisees, who were the religious leaders of the day. They liked to burden their followers with unbearable demands, but would never lift a finger to help them (Luke 11:46). Religion without Jesus will never produce the fruit of kindness.

> *In addition to the act of being useful, kindness is very much about how you make people feel.*

In addition to the act of being useful, kindness is very much about how you make people feel. People usually forget what you *say*; they frequently forget what you *do* for them; but they never forget how you made them *feel*. With the fruit of kindness, the key is to help someone in need without shaming them in the process. Some companies with excellent customer service, such as the Ritz-Carlton hotel chain, use the phrase, "My pleasure" when thanked. The act of kindness is to make someone feel that you genuinely wanted to help them.

Bible Examples of Kindness:

Ruth: She was remarkably kind to her mother-in-law, Naomi, in that she wouldn't leave her even though they'd lost everything. There was no advantage to staying with Naomi instead of returning to her own people. God rewarded Ruth's kindness by blessing her with a new husband, Boaz. Together, they were the great grandparents of King David.

Jonathan: Though at a cost, he was kind to David. Jonathan was the son of King Saul and in spite of his father's opposition towards David, he remained loyal to his friend. Jonathan certainly could have been jealous of David, like his father was. But instead he saw what God was doing in David and helped him. Jonathan said to David, "We have sworn friendship with each other in the name of the LORD" (1 Samuel 20:42 NIV).

David: Though he became king, he never failed to be kind to those under him. David was especially kind to those of Saul's household after Saul's death. *David asked, "Is there anyone still left of the house of Saul to whom I can show kindness for Jonathan's sake?"* (2 Samuel 9:1). There remained a son of Jonathan, Mephibosheth, who was lame in both feet. David restored his land and gave Mephibosheth a seat of honor at the king's dinner table each night for the rest of his life.

The Good Samaritan

Jesus gave us the parable of the Good Samaritan in order to teach us the principle of kindness (Luke 10:29-37). The religious leaders (the priest and the Levite) each passed by on the other side of the road from the wounded man. But a Samaritan showed kindness in the time of need.

> **Luke 10:33-34**
> **33 But a certain Samaritan, as he journeyed, came where he was. And when he saw him, he had compassion.**
> **34 So he went to him and bandaged his wounds, pouring on oil and wine; and he set him on his own animal, brought him to an inn, and took care of him.**

Religion and kindness don't always go together. The priest and the Levite failed. Many Christians today demonstrate these same behaviors. There can be many "spiritual" sounding excuses why we don't help people in need, but we should follow the example of the Good Samaritan when we have the opportunity to make a difference in someone else's life.

Notice that the Samaritan didn't have to go on a mission's trip to have this opportunity to make a difference. The need was there on his normal path "as he journeyed." Every day there is an opportunity to make a difference in someone's life through the gift of kindness. All of them won't be as significant as this story, but you never know what a big difference a small deed can make in another person's life.

Kindness always goes the extra mile. The Samaritan told the innkeeper, "Whatever more you spend, I will repay you when I come back" (v 35). Kindness may inconvenience you or cost you something, but the reward from the Father is so much greater than any expense of time or money.

Divine Interruptions

Much like with the God Samaritan, God will frequently bring an interruption into the life of a believer to give an opportunity to show kindness to someone in need.

Jesus was routinely interrupted in His earthly ministry by someone with a pressing need. Often the disciples would try to brush them away as if to say, "The Master has more important things to attend to." But Jesus understood the difference between a distraction and an interruption. Whether it was Zacchaeus or Bartimaeus or the Syrophoenician woman, Jesus always engaged in an opportunity to show God's kindness.

The chart below shows the difference between a *distraction* and a *divine interruption*.

Distraction	Divine Interruption
Takes your attention away from doing God's will. Leaves you feeling drained or frustrated afterwards.	Breaks into your routine or schedule to present an opportunity to be kind. Leaves you feeling refueled and refreshed afterwards.

"You Did it to Me"

> **Matthew 25:40 Assuredly, I say to you, inasmuch as you did it to one of the least of these My brethren, you did it to Me.**

Jesus makes it clear that when me meet the needs of those the world deems the least, that we are actually doing it to Him. In this passage, Jesus makes it clear that we must each give an account before Him on how we handled the opportunities to help.

Kindness Meets Needs

- Hungry → gave Me food
- Thirsty → gave Me to drink
- Stranger → took Me in
- Naked → clothed Me
- Sick → visited Me
- Prison → came to Me

God – the Ultimate Example

> **Romans 2:4 (ESV) Or do you presume on the riches of his kindness and forbearance and patience, not knowing that God's kindness is meant to lead you to repentance?**

God's kindness towards us to designed to lead us to repentance. Contrary to assumptions, there aren't many examples in the Bible where judgment led someone to repentance. Judgment is the outcome of a failure to repent, but it rarely causes someone to do a 180 turnaround. Judgment didn't make Sodom and Gomorrah repent. Judgment very

> *God's kindness towards us to designed to lead us to repentance.*

rarely caused the people of Israel to repent and it was short-lived if they did. Judgment won't make the people alive during the Great Tribulation repent (Revelation 9:21; 16:11). Please don't misunderstand; repentance will *prevent* judgment (e.g., Nineveh), but rarely will judgment cause repentance.

10. The Fruit of Goodness

*Galatians 5:22 But the fruit of the Spirit is love, joy, peace, longsuffering, kindness, **goodness**, faithfulness, 23 gentleness, self-control. Against such there is no law.*

> **Word Gem: Gr. *agathosune* (ἀγαθωσύνη) –** translated *goodness*, "the goodness that comes from God and showing itself in spiritual, moral excellence (virtue)."

The word *goodness* is in the NKJV Bible 42 times – 36 in the Old Testament and 6 in the New Testament. The word *good* is in the Bible 646 times. The word "good" is used seven times in the creation account (Genesis 1). This particular word (*agathosune*) occurs only four times in the New Testament, exclusively by the Apostle Paul. Apparently, it is strictly a biblical term. In other words, it does not seem to appear at all in secular Greek.

The fruit of goodness is unappreciated in today's world because the word "good" is used so frequently and so randomly. It's applied to just about anything. Pizza is good; jeans fit good; it was a good game. No one ever says that the pizza was longsuffering or that the pizza was patient. But God's Word has a very specific picture of what goodness is.

When I began a deeper study on this fruit called goodness, I was astonished by the amount of generic fluff that was out there. Nothing was telling me what it really meant to be good. It is like a catchall for any positive action or feeling. But the Bible definition is clear that it represents a goodness that comes from God and manifests itself in spiritual and moral excellence.

All That God Made was Good

> **Genesis 1:31 Then God saw everything that He had made, and indeed it was very good.**

Everything in God's original design was good. This is important to recognize in order to understand the nature of God. He didn't make the chaos that exists in the world today. People wrongfully blame God for every tragedy and injustice that happens.

As part of His creation, God created two important trees: the *tree of life* and the *tree of the knowledge of good and evil*. Man was forbidden to eat from the latter, while allowed to eat from every other tree in the garden. He was told that he would die if he ate from it. Yet, man had a free will. Though forbidden, he could disobey. The reason Adam was forbidden to eat from the tree was that God wanted Adam and Eve to accept His determination on what was good and evil. At that point, all was good and evil had not been allowed to penetrate Adam's world. But in Genesis chapter three, Satan deceived Eve into thinking that God was withholding something good from her and Adam. "You will be like God, knowing good and evil," Satan said (Genesis 3:4). Adam and Eve disobeyed and because of their sin, evil entered the human race and man was separated from God. All that had been created good was now corrupted with evil.

You would think that a tree called "the knowledge of good and evil" would be a good thing – giving man a greater capability to do good. But the opposite is true. Mankind doing good based on his own agenda is flawed in every aspect. The fallen nature of man is incapable of determining what is truly good or even producing the goodness if known. The Bible says that fallen man will *"call evil good, and good evil; who substitute darkness for light and light for darkness"* (Isaiah 5:20). The *tree of life* is actually is the source from which goodness flows. It allows us to see things from God's perspective and gives us the power to produce the fruit of goodness.

Redemption through the power of the cross puts goodness back into the soul of the redeemed. Yet we are still living in a broken and fallen world. This is why the fruit of goodness is so important. It allows us to represent God's kingdom to a lost world around us.

The Character of God

Throughout the Old Testament, the word *good* is used to describe the essential nature and character of God. "God is good." This thought is conveyed in the New Testament as well: "No one is good but God alone" (Mark 10:18). The idea is that only God is *completely* good. We also know that every gift from God in our lives is truly good.

> **James 1:17 Every good gift and every perfect gift is from above, and comes down from the Father of lights, with whom there is no variation or shadow of turning.**

God has never changed. He is the same God who spoke the universe into existence and deemed all of His creation to be good. The problem is that many of God's good works and gifts get obscured by the corruption that's inherent within the evil in the world. Adversity and hardship are part of the Christian's life, just like the unbeliever's. The difference is that we have God working in our situations to make a path of victory. But we must guard our hearts lest we develop an unbelieving attitude. Remember, it is imperative that we view the circumstances of our situation through the lens of God's Word and not allow the circumstances to become the lens through which we view God. He is good, all the time, and He never changes.

Good, therefore, is a condition of the heart and a state of mind, not a favorable circumstance. The fruitful life is the good life and it's based on the goodness of God, not the circumstances.

Goodness Defeats Satan

One of the primary outcomes of the fruit of goodness is the destruction of Satan's works. The goodness of God flowing through a believer defeats the kingdom of darkness. We see this in the example of Jesus' ministry.

> *Goodness is the quality that seeks to build others up and not tear them down.*

> **Acts 10:38 And you know that God anointed Jesus of Nazareth with the Holy Spirit and with power. Then Jesus went around doing good and healing all who were oppressed by the devil, for God was with him.**

Since the fall of man in the Garden of Eden, Satan has tried to stop God's goodness in the earth. He offered a counterfeit then and he sells the same lie today: "If it feels good, do it." This is deception and ultimately perpetuates the pain and suffering of humanity.

Builds Others Up

Goodness is the quality that *seeks to build others up and not tear them down*. If you stop and think, you can probably think of several people whom you love seeing. The reason is that they make you feel better about yourself. These people focus all of their energy on the positive. It's not difficult to find areas to be critical of others. Everyone has faults. The fruit of goodness allows you to see the best in other people.

Everyone loves a good boss, but they are often few and far between. When I think back on my corporate career, there were only a couple of occasions when I had what I considered a good boss. The common denominator with them was how they made their team feel important. Their encouragement and trust made you want to run through a wall for them. On the other hand, on the occasions when I had a bad boss, the boss wanted everyone to know how important he was. The results and performance of those teams was far less.

Goodness towards others will bring out the best in people.

Stretches Beyond the Ordinary

Being a doer of good stretches beyond normal or ordinary boundaries. It's a good that cannot be produced without God.

> **Matthew 5:44 But I say to you, love your enemies, bless those who curse you, <u>do good to those who hate you</u>, and pray for those who spitefully use you and persecute you.**

Not long ago, the father of a Lebanese pastor was killed by his country's Syrian enemies. Instead of seeking revenge, the pastor reached out to Syrian refugees by providing food and aid. In a recent church service, the pastor called a Syrian refugee to the front so he could wash his feet in front of the whole congregation, to remind them what it means to love and forgive. This is an extraordinary example of doing good to those this hate you.

Doing good to those who hate you does what the Bible describes as "heaping coals of fire on their head."

Proverbs 25:21-22

21 If your enemy is hungry, give him bread to eat; and if he is thirsty, give him water to drink;

22 For so you will heap coals of fire on his head, and the Lord will reward you.

Heaping coals of fire on another's head sounds pretty harsh, but in ancient Middle Eastern culture this represented sharing hot coals with neighbors on a cold morning in order for them to be warm. In spiritual terms, it allows your enemy to experience the warmth of God's love in an otherwise cold and lonely world.

Walking in the fruit of goodness is so much more than just *not doing bad*. Someone is not good, simply because he or she wasn't bad. When a mother leaves her child alone at home for a brief period and returns, she asks, "Were you a good boy"? She doesn't mean, "Did you vacuum the carpet and take out the trash." She simply wants to make sure he didn't burn the house down. God's standard of goodness, however, is much more proactive. It is not passive, but active in nature. *Do not neglect to do good and to share what you have, for such sacrifices are pleasing to God* (Hebrews 13:16).

Sharing is an essential part of goodness. The early church practiced sharing as a way of life (see Acts 2).

Hoarding is a terrible way to live; it is fear-based and ties God's hands. When the Israelites tried to hoard manna, it would be infested with maggots (Exodus 16).

The Fruit of Goodness in Daily Life

A person doesn't have to be a full-time church worker or minister in order to impact the world with the fruit of goodness. Below are some examples of ways to demonstrate goodness.

- Try to find a vocation that makes a contribution towards the good of society. This can be through the manufacturing of a product that helps people. Another example would be providing a service that helps people.

- Be a good listener. Attentive listening is a positive way to let people know that you care. Distracted listening is a way to let people know they aren't important.

- Be empathetic towards those who are suffering. Ask yourself, "How would I feel if this happened to me?" We don't have the right to decide what hurts another person.

- Put others first. Everything about the fruit of the Spirit flows from the position of putting others' needs first.

- Admit when you are wrong. Being good doesn't always mean being right. In fact, some would rather be right at the expense of being good. Goodness never feels the need to always have the leverage of being right.

There is an old saying that says, "No good deed goes unpunished." What does that mean? Simply, it means that not everyone will reciprocate gratitude for your acts of goodness. Being good and doing good must be lived out for the right reasons. Otherwise, you will become discouraged. *And let us not grow weary of doing good, for in due season we will reap, if we do not give up* (Galatians 6:9). *Due season* can mean that you reap in a different area than you sowed, at a later time.

The third triad of faithfulness, gentleness and self-control reflect our temperament in difficult circumstances.

11. The Fruit of Faithfulness

*Galatians 5:22 But the fruit of the Spirit is love, joy, peace, longsuffering, kindness, goodness, **faithfulness**, 23 gentleness, self-control. Against such there is no law.*

> Word Gem: Gr. *pistis* (πίστις) – translated *faithfulness*, "the character of one who can be relied on."

This particular word (*pistis*) shows up 244 times in the NT. The context determines the specific meaning. The majority of times, it is translated faith, which means, "conviction of the truth."

The word *pistis* is translated *faithful* in the NT 53 times and is used of persons who show themselves faithful in the transaction of business, the execution of commands, or the discharge of official duties

God is Faithful

> **1 Corinthians 10:13 No temptation has overtaken you except such as is common to**

> **man; but God is faithful, who will not allow you to be tempted beyond what you are able, but with the temptation will also make the way of escape, that you may be able to bear it.**
>
> **2 Timothy 2:13 If we are faithless, He remains faithful; He cannot deny Himself.**

In the ups and downs of life, the one thing that can be counted on is the faithfulness of God. There will be many temptations, tests and trails that assail the believer. But God is so faithful; He will not permit anything that He hasn't prepared us for in advance. The thing is, we may not yet know what we are capable of, until we get put in the situation that calls it out of us. God deposits strength, gifting and grace into our lives through various impartations. When we get tested, we see how much we've grown. As you study the Word, God is making deposits. When you pray, God is making deposits. When you go to church, God is making deposits. You don't realize how much you've grown, but when the test comes your way, you're able to make the withdrawal needed.

> *He will not permit anything that He hasn't prepared us for in advance.*

I wish I could say that through the years I've been walking with the Lord that I have always been faithful, but I can't. There are times when we are faithless as God's people. Even the 12 disciples were rebuked by Jesus for their lack of faith. *But He said to them, "Why are you fearful, O you of little faith?"* (Matthew 8:26). But even when we aren't faithful, God remains faithful to us. He cannot deny Himself.

Well Done

The words every true follower of Jesus wants to hear upon when leaving this world are, "Well done, good and faithful servant" (Matthew 25:23). It's nearly impossible to do anything well without being faithful. Taking shortcuts may lead to immediate results, but those types of results are often short-lived. God honors faithfulness. When a person is placed in a position of influence and his or her character cannot be relied on, it causes much damage to the church.

David remained faithful even when he was a fugitive on the run from King Saul. There were two occasions when he could have taken out Saul and attained the throne. But instead he did it God's way. Joseph remained faithful even when sold into slavery and later was imprisoned based on a false accusation. He could have yielded to the temptations of Potiphar's wife, but instead he wouldn't compromise. These two men were greatly honored by God and we remember them today for all the right reasons because they were faithful.

I don't want to be remembered for being unfaithful, even though I've had occasions when I was unfaithful. I don't want to be remembered as someone who quit when things got hard. In order to put unfaithful patterns behind us we must resist the temptation to quit. Some may not even realize they have a pattern of unfaithfulness. I've talked to people who thought they were completely faithful, but in reality never did anything well because they weren't faithful to see things through.

One of the reasons why people allow unfaithfulness to keep them from doing things well is the excuse, "I'm not feeling led anymore." Of course, there are occasions when God tells you to stop doing something. But if this is a regular pattern that just happens to coincide with obstacles or discouragement, there's a strong chance that you're being led by the weakness of the flesh and not the Holy Spirit.

Where To Start

Jesus outlined two very important principles as it relates to faithfulness:

1. Be faithful over the small (Luke 16:10)
2. Be faithful to help another (Luke 16:12)

Most people want to get involved with something that is established and successful. Very few are willing to get involved when things are small. But the truth is that most successful endeavors began small, but had faithful people or even just one faithful person who refused to quit. Zechariah 4:10 says, "Do not despise these small beginnings" (NLT). To *despise* means to think that something is beneath you. I know church planters who quit because their new church didn't reach a measurement of success that is predominantly worldly. Usually this comes down to the number of attendees. Everyone loves a crowd, especially when you're the one on the stage and you feel like God has given you a message. One pastor I know gave God six months to bring 100 people. He quit because he was less than halfway to the goal at the end of six months. But the question is, where did the goal come from? Was it from God? Our faithfulness should be to Him and His will, not some outward form of measurement within a defined amount of time.

Be faithful over the small and the rest of Luke 16:10 says that you will be faithful over the much, when God blesses you. The small is the testing ground for the much. Stewardship is not what you *would do* if you had more; it's what you *are doing* right now with what you have.

Further, I always tell people that if you feel called to an area of ministry, the best way to begin is to find someone who's active in that ministry and doing it well, and faithfully serve them. Jesus said that if you can be faithful in another's He will give you your own. People who sit by the phone waiting for their big break usually miss the boat. God promotes the faithful. Before I pastored my first church, there were four pastors that I faithfully served in any capacity where there was a need. I did it unto the Lord as if it were my ministry, because in reality, it was. All that we do is unto Him and for Him.

When Jacob was speaking his last words to his sons he said to Reuben, "Unstable as water, you shall not excel" (Genesis 49:4). In effect, Jacob was saying that Reuben's life would be like water that had no restraint that flowed in any and all directions. As a consequence, he would not excel. Live a life of faithfulness to the vision that God has given you. Proverbs 29:18 says, "Where there is no prophetic vision the people cast off restraint" (ESV). Have a God-ordained direction in your life and be faithful in the small areas. When you have a purpose, you'll deny yourself or use restraint in areas that don't help you fulfill your purpose.

> *Faithfulness means more than just doing the same thing over and over.*

You Can't Take The Faith Out Of Faithfulness

Faithfulness means more than just doing the same thing over and over. The Israelites wandered in the wilderness for 40 years, but they weren't faithful. They lacked the root word to faithfulness – faith. Doing something *religiously* or *routinely* when God isn't leading you is a perpetual dead-end.

It's not enough to have faith without action and it's not enough to have action without faith. Our faith must be complemented by action. This is where faith meets faithfulness.

> **James 2:17 (Berean) So too, faith by itself, if it is not complemented by action, is dead.**

Without faithfulness, there would be no "Hall of Faith" as Hebrews chapter 11 is called.

- Abel was faithful to bring an excellent sacrifice to God (v 4).
- Enoch was faithful to walk with God (v 5).
- Noah was faithful to build the ark when there was no rain (v 7).
- Abraham was faithful to leave his homeland to go to a place he didn't know (v 8).

- Abraham and Sarah were faithful for 25 years waiting on the promise of a child (v 11).

How long or how many times does one have to do something before it's considered faithful? The Bible doesn't answer that question. I'm sure Abraham had no idea that his wait would be 25 years. But at the same time, he was seeing the hand of God move in his life the whole time. It's an active waiting that causes God's hand to move. I've often said that God takes a long time to do something suddenly. It's during the *long time* that we must remain faithful or the *suddenly* will never come.

There's going to be difficult circumstances along the way, but faithfulness is the necessary ingredient to get you through. So many people quit before they see the breakthrough.

> *The reason the grass looks greener on the other side of the fence is because that person is being faithful to water it and pull weeds.*

All of the examples in the Hall of Faith could have quit before the promise was fulfilled, but they chose to believe God and remain faithful instead.

Gifting Without Faithfulness

Gifting without faithfulness will not get you very far in God's kingdom. Gifting determines ability, but faithfulness determines sustainability. Many people have been hurt by putting their trust in a leader with gifting who lacked faithfulness.

It is so clear throughout the gospels that Jesus cherishes and holds in high regard those who display the attribute of faithfulness. He knew that some would turn away because His sayings were difficult at times. His teaching didn't into the religious box of the day. There are over a dozen times when Jesus upped the ante for His followers. He started with, "Come and see" (John 1:39), but in the end, following Jesus would require laying down their lives (John 21:19). Jesus is looking for people who will be faithful to serve Him. Someone with a gift but lacks faithfulness will only last for a short while, but never reach the destination that only faithfulness can produce.

There is a great need for more faithful men and women in the church. Proverbs 20:6 says, "Most men will proclaim each his own goodness, but who can find a faithful man?" It's not about what we say we can do, or even having great abilities. What matters is are we faithful with the gifts and abilities God has given us?

Be Faithful Where You Are

The idea that the grass is greener on the other side of the fence is a myth. The truth is that God has called us to be faithful over what He's given us and if we will nurture and take care of it we will bloom where we're planted. The reason the grass looks greener on the other side of the fence is because that person is being faithful to water it and pull weeds.

When God calls you, He already knows whom you will marry, where you will live, where you will work as well as every other socioeconomic factor. Though they may seem to be, these things are not limiting factors to succeeding at God's will.

The farmer starts with a seed. It's not much to look at and serves no purpose other than going into the ground and dying. But if the farmer plants that seed and faithfully tends the ground it will bring forth much fruit (John 12:24). It's a process that requires faithfulness. Don't grow weary or become discouraged but remain faithful. The Father has perfect timing and will cause the harvest to come in due season.

> **Galatians 6:9 And let us not grow weary while doing good, for in due season we shall reap if we do not lose heart.**

12. The Fruit of Gentleness

*Galatians 5:22 But the fruit of the Spirit is love, joy, peace, longsuffering, kindness, goodness, faithfulness, 23 **gentleness**, self-control. Against such there is no law.*

> **Word Gem: Gr. *prautés* (πραΰτης) – translated *gentleness*, "the divinely balanced virtue of power and humility – meekness"**

This particular word (*prautés*) shows up nine times in the New Testament. Some Bible versions translate the word as *meekness*. Meekness is often misconstrued as weakness, but as can be seen from the meaning, that is far from the truth. It is the divinely balanced virtue of power and humility.

Strength Under Control

The Greek word *prautés* comes from the root word of *praus* (used three times), which was the Greek word used to describe war horses. The powerful war horse was always under the control of its master, even though it had tremendous power and ability. When the horse was trained and it got to the place where it would obey its master under any conditions, it was then deemed suitable for battle. Even though it had this great power and capacity, it would yield and submit to its master.

An engineer by the name of James Watt was inspired by the strength of the horse when he came up with the term "horsepower" as a new unit of measurement. Watt guessed that a horse could lift 33,000 pounds exactly one foot in one minute. Even though it wasn't based upon any precise calculations, it still stands as a popular measurement today.

> *Being meek or gentle doesn't mean that you allow everyone to push you around.*

As individuals made in the image of God, we have been given tremendous abilities to think, work, invent, feel and communicate. This is all given with free will, meaning that we may each live our lives as we choose. When we come to Jesus and experience the new birth, we are given the power of the Holy Spirit. Along with that power come spiritual gifts. Combined, each of us has a vast assortment of natural and spiritual gifts. In other words, we each have a lot of *horsepower*.

It's what we do with that horsepower that determines whether we live fruitfully or not. Like the war horse, to be meek and gentle is to "have great strength and power that is under control of the Master." Keep in mind that just anyone couldn't order this kind of horse around, but just its master. Being meek or gentle doesn't mean that you allow everyone to push you around. But it does mean that you are under the Lord's control and He may guide you and lead you as He desires.

This same word is found in the beatitudes.

> **Matthew 5:5 Blessed are the meek [praus], for they shall inherit the earth.**

The fruitful life is the yielded life. When we surrender our lives to Jesus, we relinquish our rights at act independently. This can be a difficult concept to grasp for some Christians. But Jesus said, *"If anyone desires to come after Me, let him deny himself, and take up his cross, and follow Me"* (Matthew 16:24). This denial of one's self really isn't thinking less of one's self, but rather thinking of one's self less.

> *The whole Christian walk is a paradox from the world's ways.*

The whole Christian walk is a paradox from the world's ways. In order to gain, one must lose. In order to be great, one must be a servant. The old nature's instinct is to self-defend and self-promote. But the new nature is secure in Him. This security and identity in Christ gives us the inner contentment so that we don't have to promote or defend ourselves.

The type of gentleness the Bible describes is what we learn from the Lord, through relationship with Him. Jesus was the perfect example of the divine balance of power and humility. Matthew 11:29 says, *"Take My yoke upon you and learn from Me, for I am gentle and lowly in heart, and you will find rest for your souls."* Notice that Jesus said to "learn from Me," not "learn about Me." If all one does is learn *about* Jesus, there is no transformation. There is true rest that comes into my soul when I discover that I don't have to push my way forward and make my own way. Yielded to Him, I allow the Lord to make the way and I follow.

Gentleness Restores

With so many broken lives all around us, gentleness is a necessary ingredient to help people. Coming at them with harshness will only drive them further into shame and brokenness. Galatians 6:1 lays it out perfectly:

> **Galatians 6:1 Brethren, if a man is overtaken in any trespass, you who are spiritual restore such a one in a spirit of gentleness,**

considering yourself lest you also be tempted.

Found in this verse are some very helpful truths to consider with regards to who is able to help one who is overtaken by a trespass.

1. **The person must be a spiritual person.** People measure spirituality by all sorts of ways. Some times it's by how much better or godlier they are than other people. But here, the Bible says that a spiritual person will be involved in restoring broken people. This is one of the ways we know that the Pharisees weren't spiritual people because they never tried to help the broken. In fact, their self-righteousness contributed to the broken condition of others.

2. **The motivation must be restoration.** It's not hard to point out other people's failures. The tendency is to judge others by their actions and judge ourselves by our intentions. Most people who get overtaken by sin didn't set out for it to happen. In fact, the original word for *overtaken* means "to be taken by surprise." Condemning people just pushes them further into their shame. Everything, even correction, must be done for the purpose of restoration.

3. **Restoration must be done in a spirit of gentleness.** Even though you have the ability to

crush the person who's overtaken, instead you don't use that power. Through a spirit of gentleness, you seek to restore. Your gentle spirit doesn't excuse the sin, but understands that the consequences have already exacted a heavy toll. Jesus told the woman caught in adultery, "Neither do I condemn you; go and sin no more" (John 8:11).

4. **The person must consider him or herself in order to avoid temptation.** As the saying goes, your sin always looks worse when you see someone else doing it. The Christian must always guard the heart. Pride is very deceptive and always goes before a fall (Proverbs 18:12). There is no one above temptation. To consider yourself means *to be attentive*. Make sure that you are keeping yourself spiritually filled so that you're able to help others.

The Hidden Person of the Heart

True gentleness is not something that one can feign. Adverse circumstances will expose its absence. Gentleness is an attribute of the spirit – the part of you that's hidden inside. This is where all of the fruit of the Spirit is developed.

> **1 Peter 3:4 Rather let it be the hidden person of the heart, with the incorruptible beauty of**

a gentle and quiet spirit, which is very precious in the sight of God.

The fruitful life comes from the invisible part of your life. The real you is hidden – it is your spirit. People usually focus on what they can see in the natural. For example, if you lose weight, everyone notices and compliments you. Physically attractive people are assumed to *have it all together*. But that beauty is corruptible; it's going to fade. True and incorruptible beauty comes from a spirit that's gentle and quiet. The word quiet in the original Greek (*hésuchios*) means, "Quiet (still) and steady (settled) due to a divinely-inspired inner calmness."

> *The fruitful life comes from the invisible part of your life. The real you is hidden – it is your spirit.*

The context of the above verse is in relation to a believing wife winning her unbelieving husband to the Lord. She is able to win him to the Lord through her conduct, led by a gentle and quiet spirit.

A Gentle Answer

Gentleness is most often revealed through our words. There is great power in the words we speak to others – not just the actual words, but also the tone in which they're spoken. Actually, studies have shown that only

7% of communication is spoken words, but 38% is the tone of voice and 55% body language.

> **Proverbs 15:1 (NIV) A gentle answer turns away [deflects] wrath, but a harsh word stirs up anger.**

It can be difficult for the human temperament to let things go. The need to be right or be heard can cause someone to lose focus on what's really important. Some times it's more important to hear than to be heard. Other times I need to process things healthily before I speak.

We are living in an age where comments have taken the place of conversation. Everyone has a platform through social media for their voice to be heard. Before hitting *send*, think about the consequences. Will your comment deflect anger or will it stir it up?

When speaking into another person's life there are two things to keep in mind:

1. **How much is the person ready to receive?** There were times when the Lord had to hold back from the disciples because they weren't ready to receive everything that could've been said (John 16:12).

2. **What is it that the Holy Spirit wants me to say?** The Holy Spirit knows the behind-the-scenes situation. Don't lean on your own understanding (Proverbs 3:5-6).

The fruit of gentleness will save relationships, heal the brokenhearted and restore the fallen. It is not just what you do, but *how* you do it.

13. The Fruit of Self-Control

*Galatians 5:22 But the fruit of the Spirit is love, joy, peace, longsuffering, kindness, goodness, faithfulness, 23 gentleness, **self-control**. Against such there is no law.*

> **Word Gem: Gr.** *egkrateia* (ἐγκράτεια) – translated *self-control*, "dominion within"

This particular word (*egkrateia*) appears four times in the New Testament. The root word (*kratos*) means, "dominion, power, strength or mastery." The prefix (*eg*) indicates that it comes from *within*. Every time the word is used, it is always within the context of a fruit of the Spirit. Self-control (*egkrateia*) is never mentioned as a discipline that can be attained by human determination. HELPS Word Studies describes it this way: *self-control – proceeding out from within oneself, but not by oneself.*

While the world uses flattering *self*-hyphenated words such as self-help, self-image and self-worth, the Bible uses a different perspective. The Bible uses *self-*

hyphenated words such as self-control, self-discipline and self-denial. On the surface, that seems very negative. Does God want me to be down on myself? Not exactly. It's simply that the self-help, self-image and self-worth culture of the world is looking to the wrong source. All that a person can do on their own will still come short and leave a person separated from God.

Even though this fruit is called *self-control*, this type of self-control does not *originate* from self, but rather the Holy Spirit who indwells the believer. This fruit pertains to self but does not come from self. This is where the principle of *self-help* will fail you because the help does not come *from* yourself. As with the previous eight fruit, this fruit is the supernatural manifestation of the character of Jesus being formed in you and ultimately flowing out from you.

> *Even though this fruit is called self-control, this type of self-control does not originate from self.*

Self-control is the ability to restrain one's emotions, desires, speech and behaviors and to be in harmony with God's will.

The Flesh is Powerless

Romans chapter 7 describes the condition of one who desires and wills to do what is right, but ultimately does what is against his wishes. It is a powerless condition that one lives without Christ.

> **Romans 7:18-20**
> **18 For I know that in me (that is, in my flesh) nothing good dwells; for to will is present with me, but how to perform what is good I do not find.**
> **19 For the good that I will to do, I do not do; but the evil I will not to do, that I practice.**
> **20 Now if I do what I will not to do, it is no longer I who do it, but sin that dwells in me.**

The flesh, as mentioned in the Bible, is the selfish orientation of the old nature. So even though the selfish orientation wants something that is ultimately good for self, it is completely powerless to make it happen. Self-help programs cannot change the old fallen nature. The *want* is there but the *how* is beyond reach. Some people think that will power is enough. Even though strong will power is useful, it will only take you so far.

Paul, in verse 20, brings out the truth that if we are incapable of doing the good that we desire, it is because of the power of sin. Paul is not referring to a single act of sin or a single sinful behavior pattern.

Rather, he is referring to the sin nature that every single person is born with. When you get born again, God gives you a new nature (2 Corinthians 5:21). But we must keep in mind that every day we must *put off* the old self and *put on* the new self.

> **Ephesians 4:22-24**
> **22 to put off your old self, which belongs to your former manner of life and is corrupt through deceitful desires,**
> **23 and to be renewed in the spirit of your minds,**
> **24 and to put on the new self, created after the likeness of God in true righteousness and holiness.**

The fruit of self-control can only come from the new self, formed in the image of Christ. The new self is *put on* by the renewing of the mind with the Word of God (see also Romans 12:2). So, while the Holy Spirit produces the fruit of self-control, He needs our active participation in order to exercise the fruit. We can't indulge all of our impulses and say, "I guess I didn't get the gift." The Holy Spirit cannot deny self for us, but He can do it through us.

> *The fruit of self-control can only come from the new self, formed in the image of Christ.*

The very concept of self-control indicates that there is a battle within. There is a part of self that needs denied or controlled. Some would suppose that with hard work, lots of prayer and Bible study, this divided self would go away. Yet we are told that denying ourselves would be a daily exercise as long as we follow Jesus.

> **Luke 9:23 Then He said to them all, "If anyone desires to come after Me, let him deny himself, and take up his cross daily, and follow Me.**

The Boundary of Self-Control

The fruit of self-control is a God-given gift in the form of a boundary. There are many boundaries associated with our relationship with God. For example, nature is a boundary that protects us through our instincts. God's Word is a boundary that is designed to guide us into truth and protect us from evil. The fruit of self-control is another level of boundary given to us from God to protect us from the harm of excess. The desires of self, if unrestrained, will lead to destruction. Some think of boundaries as a form of punishment, but God gives boundaries in order to protect us. Through the fruit of self-control a believer is able to flourish.

Different Levels of Boundaries

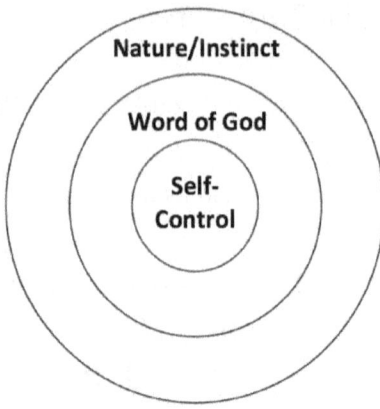

No to the Flesh & Yes to the Spirit

A person who cannot restrain his emotions and must always speak his mind is of very limited use in the kingdom of God.

> **James 1:19 Know this, my beloved brothers: let every person be quick to hear, slow to speak, slow to anger.**

According to 2 Peter 1:6, *knowledge* must come before self-control. The old adage is that knowledge is power, and in this case, that is so. As you grow in your knowledge of the Lord, through His Word, the *dominion within* increases.

These are some areas that self-control is very helpful:

- Words (the tongue)
- Appetite
- Spending
- Parenting
- Screen time (TV, PC, Smartphone)
- Spiritual disciplines (prayer, Bible reading)
- Emotions

Self-control empowers us to say 'no' to the flesh and 'yes' to the Spirit.

Self-Discipline

Working in conjunction with self-control is self-discipline.

> **1 Corinthians 9:24-27**
>
> **24 Do you not know that those who run in a race all run, but one receives the prize? Run in such a way that you may obtain it.**
>
> **25 And everyone who competes for the prize is temperate in all things. Now they do it to obtain a perishable crown, but we for an imperishable crown.**
>
> **26 Therefore I run thus: not with uncertainty. Thus I fight: not as one who beats the air.**

27 But I discipline my body and bring it into subjection, lest, when I have preached to others, I myself should become disqualified.

Other Important Verses Dealing With The Fruitful Life

Psalm 1:3 He shall be like a tree Planted by the rivers of water, That brings forth its fruit in its season, Whose leaf also shall not wither; And whatever he does shall prosper.

Psalm 92:14 They shall still bear fruit in old age; They shall be fresh and flourishing,

Matthew 3:10 And even now the ax is laid to the root of the trees. Therefore every tree which does not bear good fruit is cut down and thrown into the fire.

Matthew 7:16-20 You will know them by their fruits. Do men gather grapes from thornbushes or figs from thistles? 17 Even so, every good tree bears good fruit, but a bad tree bears bad fruit. 18 A good tree cannot bear bad fruit, nor can a bad tree bear good fruit. 19 Every tree that does not bear good fruit is cut down and thrown into the fire. 20 Therefore by their fruits you will know them.

Luke 3:8 Therefore bear fruits worthy of repentance.

John 15:16 You did not choose Me, but I chose you and appointed you that you should go and bear fruit, and that your fruit should remain, that whatever you ask the Father in My name He may give you.

Romans 6:22 But now having been set free from sin, and having become slaves of God, you have your fruit to holiness, and the end, everlasting life.

Ephesians 5:9 for the fruit of the Spirit is in all goodness, righteousness, and truth.

Philippians 1:11 being filled with the fruits of righteousness which are by Jesus Christ, to the glory and praise of God.

Philippians 4:17 Not that I seek the gift, but I seek the fruit that abounds to your account.

Colossians 1:10 that you may walk worthy of the Lord, fully pleasing Him, being fruitful in every good work and increasing in the knowledge of God;

Hebrews 12:11 Now no chastening seems to be joyful for the present, but painful; nevertheless, afterward it yields the peaceable fruit of righteousness to those who have been trained by it.

James 3:17 But the wisdom that is from above is first pure, then peaceable, gentle, willing to yield, full of mercy and good fruits, without partiality and without hypocrisy.

Other Books by David Chapman

All books may be purchased through Amazon

Thy Word: A Devotional Commentary on Psalm 119 Apr 17, 2019
by David A. Chapman
Paperback
$10⁰⁰ ✓prime

Other Formats: Kindle Edition

The Power of Praise: The 7 Hebrew Words for Praise May 27, 2014
by David Chapman
Paperback
$10⁰⁰ ✓prime

Other Formats: Kindle Edition

The Believer's Deliverance Handbook: 7 Levels of Demonic Involvement and How to Minister Deliverance
Jan 29, 2014
by David Chapman
Paperback
$7⁰⁰ ✓prime

Other Formats: Kindle Edition

Caught Up: The Rapture of the Church Jun 24, 2015
by David Chapman
Paperback
$10⁰⁰ ✓prime

Other Formats: Kindle Edition

Modern Day Apostles: The Supernatural Ministry of the Apostle in the Modern Day Church Mar 4, 2014
by David Chapman
Paperback
$10⁰⁰ ✓prime

Other Formats: Kindle Edition

The Kingdom Within Aug 17, 2016
by David Chapman
Paperback
$9⁷⁸ $12.00 ✓prime

Other Formats: Kindle Edition

Knowing God's Will: & Walking in His Blessing Nov 15, 2014
by David Chapman
Paperback
$10⁰⁰ ✓prime

Other Formats: Kindle Edition , Mass Market Paperback

The Power of the Anointing Dec 7, 2014
by David Chapman
Paperback
$10⁰⁰ ✓prime

Other Formats: Kindle Edition

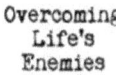

Overcoming Life's Enemies Sep 10, 2016
by David Chapman
Paperback
$10⁰⁰ ✓prime

Other Formats: Kindle Edition

Unlocking the Power of Honor Aug 9, 2018
by David Chapman
Paperback
$10⁰⁰ ✓prime

Counted Faithful: Verse-by-Verse Commentary on I Timothy Jun 1, 2017
by Dr. David Chapman
Paperback
$12⁰⁰ ✓prime

Other Formats: Kindle Edition

The Pattern & The Glory: The New Testament Pattern for the Glorious End-Time Church Jul 30, 2015
by David Chapman
Paperback
$12.00 prime

Other Formats: Kindle Edition

Thus Saith The Lord: Prophecy & Tongues May 15, 2014
by David Chapman
Paperback
$8.00 prime

Other Formats: Kindle Edition

The Seven Letters of Jesus: God's Message to the End-Time Church Nov 16, 2015
by David A Chapman
Paperback
$10.00 prime

Other Formats: Kindle Edition

The Fullness of the Spirit: How to be Filled with the Holy Spirit & Walk in Victory Feb 26, 2014
by David A Chapman
Paperback
$10.00 prime

Other Formats: Kindle Edition

Blood Covenant: The Power of the Blood of Jesus Feb 3, 2014
by David Chapman
Paperback
$10⁰⁰ ✓prime

Other Formats: Kindle Edition

You may contact David Chapman by writing to:

TRU Publishing
1726 S. 1st Ave.
Safford, Arizona 85546

Or by emailing:
TheRiverAZ@gmail.com

www.ingramcontent.com/pod-product-compliance
Lightning Source LLC
Chambersburg PA
CBHW030621070426
42449CB00041B/906